A
Dream
Come True

D1388081

A Dream Come True

(A Devotional Study of Psalm 126)

Angus MacKinnon

Catalone Press

Acknowledgment

I wish to acknowledge my gratitude to my wife Mary for her help and encouragement in preparing and proofreading the manuscript for printing.

ISBN 0-9698337-0-9

Published by the Catalone Press,
P.O. Box 1878, Sydney Nova Scotia

Printed by City Printers, Sydney, N.S.

Cover Picture: Little Narrows, Cape Breton, Nova Scotia.

To the memory of my mother
Catherine Matheson MacKinnon
of Stoer, Assynt, Scotland

CONTENTS

Introduction

The Book of Psalms is the Supermarket for the soul. All who long for a balanced life, where the negatives of our nature are changed into dynamic power, are invited to do their spiritual shopping in this Outlet of the Scriptures, which God has provided for our life journey here.

This book is part of a series of devotional studies of the Psalms. In this study of Psalm 126 the individual and collective needs of human beings are mirrored in the historic setting of the return of the Hebrews from captivity in Babylon (Iraq), during the governorship of Nehemiah and the prophet Ezra. We are indebted to both Nehemiah and Ezra for their journalistic descriptions of the dramatic events which followed the people's return to their homeland and their spiritual heritage.

Psalm 126 suggests that this return was like a 'dream come true' for one and all. Old and young wept as they found again their roots and their lost heritage. We are told that the new consciousness of being God's people was so compulsive that the people persuaded the ministers to extend the services of worship, because of the joy of learning again the precious teachings of God's Law and God's Love.

As Israel in all its evolutionary history is surely the prototype of the Church of Christ in the wider sphere of the world family, so the Psalm before us is also for you and me, and all who yearn for inward joy and outward peace in the true and complete liberation of mankind.

Arnish, Cape Breton   Angus MacKinnon
1994

1. When the Lord turned again the captivity of Zion, we were like them that dream.

2. Then was our mouth filled with laughter, and our tongue with singing; then said they among the heathen, The Lord hath done great things for them.

3. The Lord hath done great things for us; whereof we are glad.

4. Turn again our captivity, O Lord, as the streams in the south.

5. They that sow in tears shall reap in joy.

6. He that goeth forth and weepeth, bearing precious seed, shall doubtless come again with rejoicing, bringing his sheaves with him.

(Psalm 126)

1

Elective Love

The bay was dotted with hardy working vessels, coastal schooners with booms hanging over their sterns, small fishing -boats, gaff cutters and sloops. There was an air of serenity and order. Things were as they should be, where men of the sea awaited a new spring with all its hopes and expectations. In a boat-yard nearby sat pleasure-boats covered with canvas, bowsprits peeping out of their shelters, and varnished spruce or pine spars lying on trestles nearby. Already there was a stirring after the winter rest. Soon the fishing boats would be joined by the pleasure-boats, making Fairhaven the idyllic setting for a summer holiday by the sea.

In a field near the estuary of the Acushnet river, close to the grave of John Cook, a revered Pilgrim Father, lay an old boat, its hull weathered and worn, its planking sprung at the shoulders, the spars lying rotting on the ground, and remnants of the old sails tangled with ropes and blocks, hanging over the gunwale— a forlorn reminder of a once proud little ship. A close look would reveal some writing on the transom. The paint had long gone, but the name had been chiselled into the wood. SPRAY, BOSTON. The 'Spray' was a has-been. Her sailing days were over. The world now passed her by and eventually the earth itself would swallow her up, recycled according to nature's law. So everyone thought, if they thought at all, about the 'Spray', until this cold March day, when Joshua Slocum looked at the tired old hull. So this was the boat a friend had given to him as a gift. With the eyes of a world-travelled captain who was also an accomplished shipwright, Joshua Slocum saw a totally different picture from that of the ordinary observer. He had a vision in his mind of the Spray coming alive again. He envisaged the old sloop reborn, her mast bending to the wind and her bow dipping to the swell; he could see her crossing oceans and making a landfall in sunny lands. The dream was there, the vision of glorious possibilities. Passive, submissively, the old boat lay there in the field, waiting as it were, not for a funeral pyre to mark its final demise, but rather, for its rebirth, its rebuilding, its recommissioning, with a captain and a course and a 'star to steer her by'.

His fellow captains laughed when Slocum began re-building the old oystercatcher. The fact is, Slocum fell in love with the 'Spray'. He resolved to make her completely new.

You see, every part of her was there but every part of her had to be replaced and renewed. And that's what Joshua Slocum did. He rebuilt the Spray right up from the keel and he used the pasture oak tree nearby to make the stem. Within a year the Spray was launched, and in the annals of the sea the Spray of Boston has a place of honour, alongside America's 'Constitution', England's 'Victory', or Scotland's 'Cutty Sark'. In the Spray, Joshua Slocum, of Nova Scotia sailed round the world, alone, thus making maritime history.

The hundred year old oyster-catcher rotting in the field became a new boat, and with its winged canvas, flew across the world's oceans, achieving immortality, making a 'dream come true'.

God does the same thing for you and me. In effect he finds us when our life seems finished, a write-off, cast up on the beach of life, spent and even in our own eyes, rotten to the core. Redeeming people is God's speciality, making us completely new, right up from the keel, like the old Spray. And when God makes us completely new, he launches us, not to swing at anchor in the shallows of life in a safe easy existence of self interest. Rather He has a dream for us to fulfil, a dream to share with 'the people of God' in the continuing fulfilment of history, with our lives and our voyage of faith as an essential and glorious part in our generation. You can understand how essential it is for us to be made completely new, if you think of the Spray. She could never make the voyage round the world without a complete overhaul and renewal. Slocum rebuilt her completely, exactly according to her original dimensions, only adding extra high bulwarks, considered necessary for ocean sailing. She was legally still the original Spray, according to the maritime authority of Lloyd's Register, but in effect the Spray was a new creation, made ready to fulfil her true destiny, and share the dream of her master and captain, Joshua Slocum. She was a new creation. She was born again.

Those who have to do with boats know the language of the sea; they speak of stems and rudders, masts and goosenecks, turnbuckles and dead-eyes, heel and stability, variation and deviation. When God 'finds' us or when we 'find' Him and when all the theory of religion becomes a reality in our lives, in the union of our wills and the submissiveness of our hearts, the work of the Holy Spirit transforms us from being a spent run-down wreck, into a vibrant new creation.

New words are now part of our vocabulary. We now have a mind for spiritual things. Sometimes a great amount of vocabulary is actually latent in the forgotten compartments of our memory, lying dormant from periods of our life when we were taught Scriptural and religious knowledge. We never before had a taste for that. But when grace has touched our hearts and the love of Christ in his redeeming work makes us part of the 'great dream', we have a new language. Most of it comes from the Scriptures. We speak of guilt but also of pardon; of sin, but also of salvation; of backsliding but also of restoration. We are introduced into a new world of grace which signifies the infinite resources of the living God.

This means that Christ and His finished work on Calvary become for us the very fulcrum of history and the pivotal point of our lives. We now speak of saving grace and the therapy of 'coming to the throne of grace'. We become familiar with transactions with heaven, where instead of nursing grievances against God and our neighbours, or burning ourselves out with self-destructive guilt trips, we rejoice as we speak of mercy and grace for every time and every kind of need. We learn the language of dynamic living, where faith in Christ Jesus and his unsearchable riches enables us to reach out, to overcome, to be more than conquerors through Him that loved us. There is no ambiguity. We know Him whom we have believed and when He has rebuilt us like the old 'Spray', right up from the keel, and launched us, we are in the 'dream' business, the kind in which the dreams come true and our life now is lived by faith in the Son of God.

It is said that love makes the world go round. It is also true that it is love that turns things around for anyone in this world. When God sets his love on you, then you become the object of his rebuilding program. Everyone has to be made ready for the realisation of the dream. The life of faith, with all the challenges of the Christian witness, is a survival course as well as one of thrills and achievement.

The log of the Christian journey is often one of overcoming great adversity, enduring hardship, being helped by other travellers, being saved from shipwreck. Yes, even the log of the Spray, sailed by Slocum, the great sea captain, records these and other experiences in her three year voyage around the world.

This is what Psalm 126 is all about, a people who came back to their heritage, who found again their God-given destiny, who found that life as God's people, personally and collectively, exceeded their wildest dreams. And in turn the Christian church, of which Israel's history is the prototype, has room for all who want to 'find' life and to realise the 'great dream' of Christ, who has fulfilled the Father's redemptive will for a fallen world. Let us trace that invitation of grace from its very source in the heart of God.

Be still and let the outstretched arm lay hold upon you. Let Him replace every rotten plank right down to the keel, as Slocum did with the old 'Spray'. And let God build you into a new creation, fully restored from top to toe. Then think about it all, the wonder of what the Lord has done. It all begins at the source, what we might call the elective love of God.

No person whose heart has once been touched by the Eternal, can be really happy in any place or situation which is marked clearly 'of the world' and 'of time'. There are people, many thousands, who appear to be adjusted to the world and appear to be regulated by a philosophy of time, and yet who are out of place. These are marked out for heaven.

God in His varied providences calls them with the dynamic authority of His Spirit, to come out, to come back, to return, to repent, to come home.

Even as the century draws to a close and another century already appears on the horizon, there is scarcely any part of the world where people can avoid hearing from a transistor radio the call to return to God, to 'seek the Lord while He is to be found and to call upon Him while He is near' (Isaiah 55:6).

God's Love ELECTS but does not SELECT

The elective love of God which is set upon those who are saved, does not exclude anyone. Some people would excuse their own passive unresponsiveness to God's call by saying that God is selective. But that is not so. God does not cream off the best; He does not discriminate.

> *For God so loved the world, that whosoever believeth on Him should not perish, but have everlasting life.*
> (John 3:16)

> *Ho every one that thirsteth, come ye to the waters, and he that hath no money; come ye, buy, and eat; yea, come, buy wine and milk without money and without price.* (Isaiah 55:1)

No one can know the mind of God in His elective love, for God's thoughts are higher than the heavens above us. But we do know this, that his mercy is just as great. To select belongs to man, and can apply to the wisdom God gives His church in the deployment of gifts or people, in situations of service where we can speak of 'calls' and appointments to office. Selection belongs to function. But election, namely the election to salvation by God who calls sinners from all eternity, can only be by God, and Scripture gives no instance that this is selection.

Some would attack God, imputing selection to Him, making this an excuse for not returning to God, for remaining in sin, for staying in the company of the world, for making their permanent home in Babylon, turning their back on God's Elective Love.

Isaiah was definitely a Gospel writer when He saw God's elective love reaching out to the ends of the earth. Listen to the international note:

> ...*Nations that knew not Thee, shall run*
> *unto Thee, because of the Lord thy God,*
> *and for the Holy One of Israel; for He*
> *hath glorified thee.*

(Isaiah 55:5)

How then, you ask, do some people come back to God, as if they were coming home? How is it that they are stirred up out of an apparent complacency, and begin to seek the Lord, abandon material goals, and join God's people and God's Cause? This is a critical point, the junction of God's elective love and a sinner's will. Here is the dovetailing of Divine desire and the desire of the yearning and the longing soul, which can never be satisfied until it rests in the Everlasting Arms of a Mighty Redeemer. This is the decisive point which, if there is a positive outcome, will be indelibly written in the diary of everyone who shall yet appear in Zion at last, whose portion is with the saints, who has shares in Glory.

Even as you read this, I do not know where you stand, what makes your life tick, what are your goals, what direction you are taking. Maybe your life is like an old spring watch which has to be wound up every day, or like the latest solar-powered watch, which keeps going forever, as long as it gets normal sunshine. If your life is like the latter, being exposed to the rays of the Sun of Righteousness, even Christ the Lord, then, indeed, you have the power of the Eternal and life everlasting. What a glorious salvation which rests upon the Elective Love of God.

The Response of Faith

> *But without faith it impossible to please Him [God]: for he that cometh to God must believe that He is, and that He is the rewarder of them that diligently seek Him.* (Hebrews 11:6)

Faith is the positive response you and I make to God's saving call. You do not need to analyse it before you use it, any more than you need a course in mechanics before you learn to drive a car. Nor can faith be put in a set sequence among other factors in the spiritual equation, to fit every believer's experience.

And further, we are not convinced that it is beneficial to claim that faith must be conceived in a particular system of theology or fine logic. Faith is reasonable but it is not reason. When we come to God in faith, God does not ask us, 'Why are you here?' He doesn't tap us on the shoulder and ask, 'How did you get in?' or 'What business have you being here in my presence?'

God is no respecter of persons. He does not see nor judge as man sees or judges. He takes us as we are. You see He has the resources in the unsearchable riches of Christ to make us completely new, 'without money and without price'.

God takes all the thoughts and the emotions in our heart, as they fill our consciousness, and puts them in order. You can well realise this, if you think of a preacher declaring the truths of the Gospel, from the negative darkness of sin to the efficacy of the redeeming power of the Resurrection of Jesus, the Christ. Just think of all the different impressions these truths make upon a receptive mind. The soul then stirs right inside the heart. It is awakened through the light of the truth communicating to it through the mind. Here is a crucial point. The Lord is seeking a lost soul. The lost soul is seeking the Lord. A saving God meets a seeking soul. There is a tumult of thought, there is an agitation of emotion, and the soul is crying out for release. It is presented with this picture of many contradictions, of thoughts and emotions.

The Spiritual Equation

It is here the will of the person becomes affected by heaven's power. Holy desires fill the heart as the soul thirsts like a deer for water. What takes place at this point is a glorious transaction between a soul and God. The necessary parts are there for a saving encounter. All it requires is the dynamic power to bring the encounter to be sealed.

The Magnetic Power of Christ

It is then, even as the soul yearns, that the power of heaven through the Holy Spirit, pervades the mind. If you saw a sheet of white paper covered with small iron filings, all these separate little iron filings would appear scattered over the paper without any order. Now if you hold a magnet under the sheet of paper, a wonderful thing happens. All the little iron filings move so that they form a pattern. You see, they become magnetised and the chaos and disorder are replaced by a wonderful relationship which can be identified and photographed.

Spiritual Factors: The mind, the will, the heart, the soul

In the response of faith, as we believe in God and in the saving work of Christ, God's power magnetises the factors, and integrates them into a relationship with Christ, where His redeeming merits are laid hold of by the soul. The will is welded to the saving will of God's elective love.

From there on, exquisite joy, peace, yes, and salvation in all its dynamic efficacy flow to the soul. The mind becomes the willing servant of the soul. The heart with all the emotions becomes the location for the enthronement of Christ. The soul is animated with adoration for Him who is truly 'the chief among ten thousand and the altogether lovely one' (Song of Solomon 5: 10, 16).

God knows us, in His elective will, before we come to Him

God knows us before we hear of Him, even as Jesus told the despised tax collector Zaccheus, that He knew him while he was still perched up in the sycamore tree. God's love is so great that 'whosoever' is welcome, but it must be 'whosoever will'. It doesn't matter how far gone we are; it doesn't matter though our sins are 'as scarlet'. Remember, 'He is able to save to the uttermost them that come unto God by him...' (Hebrews 7:25).

When we realise this, we go forward stumbling, weeping, penitent, maybe unable to articulate the tumult, the excitement in our heart. We know only this, that the power of heaven is drawing us, that all the love we had for the world, for all the things that once we craved, all the transitory and earthly things that had seemed so desirable, all the love for these has given way to a new overpowering love, even the 'love of Christ that passeth knowledge' (Eph 3:19).

How do you know that anyone has returned to God? The answer is that the evidence will be seen in his or her life. People who have by faith laid hold upon a Living Saviour, will no longer be found in the 'tents of sin', will no longer seek the company of evildoers. Their lives will change in all aspects. I remember a man who was known to use profane language. After his conversion, his language became different. His last words to me were these, 'Preach to people on the obstacles that keep them from Christ.' That is reasonable.

Faith is something living, a spiritual membrane that links a soul to God through Christ, the crucified and risen Lord. Faith brings one to the footstool of God, and that is, to the feet of Christ, now set down at the right hand of the Father. The touch of heaven on the believer's soul, the glimpse of the stripes with which we are healed, the breath of heaven, as the Spirit whispers that God has chosen us, fill our hearts to overflowing.

All this is glorious. Such intercourse with heaven rejoices the heart. This is the unspeakable intimacy between a needy soul and an all-sufficient Saviour. This is the 'idea' that is beyond the power of language to express. My friend, this is bigger than the individual. When our hearts are full and as sinners we rest in the 'everlasting arms', when we lean upon our beloved, there is a glorious sense of the collective. People are not shut out of such an experience. Rather God's interest is in the multitudes, so that heaven will be full at the banquet of Christ and His Church. And the individual is now part of this. He says with the church, 'My Beloved is mine, and I am His' (Song of Solomon 2:16).

2

A State of Grace

The person who responds in faith is now in a state of grace. He reflects, he meditates on God's Law, he thinks and muses on the wonderful way in which God has led him in His providence and by His Word. His faith all seems so reasonable, that he wonders how blind he had been to all the gracious overtures of a loving Saviour. He rejoices as he sees it all, as he traces Elective Love seeking him out and never giving up until he closed in with Christ and His saving offer in the Covenant of Grace. He sees it all now. His faith is the expression of the effectual Word of God. Faith is linked with the Word that goes out. Without the Word going out, the sinner to be redeemed cannot hear. But when the free Gospel of redeeming love is heard, those who will, respond and return. Elective Love lays hold on them and will not let them go.

The Power of the Word

The Word is powerful and cannot return without completing its redeeming work. There is nothing like this, people returning, drawn by Elective Love. They are there in all history in every generation, in every continent, in the city and in the countryside, in the plain and in the mountain. Day and night through the ages, there is this continuous caravan of people, who hear the call of heaven and return to God by way of the Cross.

Without the Word going forth, people remain in darkness. They may appear at peace with themselves and others, but that is an illusion. I think of a country like Japan, with its ancient religious culture, as its people are carried forward in the economic fusion of technology and Western inventiveness. Already there is a change in the technological picture. The Japanese are themselves becoming the initiators or leaders in new ideas, at one time seen as almost synonymous with the Western world.

Wait and see. It may well be that there will also be a change in the spiritual sphere. Already as we write towards the end of the 20th century, there is a restlessness as individual souls become uneasy in the collective acquiescence without God. That very acquiescence of group tolerance could lead in the coming century to mass conversions, unparalleled since the conversion of the Roman Empire.

The Message of Freedom

Let the Word go out. Let the Church proclaim it to the ends of the earth. Let Zion declare that God is exalted, that the Redeemer is mighty. Let the message be heard on all wavelengths, 'Jesus Christ the Saviour of the world'. Then 'whosoever will' will respond. That is faith. There is no need to explain to God. There is no need to write for an appointment at the throne of grace. There is no need to get your request for mercy typed out. Come with the tear-stained confession and let it be like this; 'Father I have sinned against heaven and in thy sight', or 'Lord be merciful to me a sinner', or 'Lord, remember me when thou comest into thy kingdom'.

Focus all thoughts upon Christ

When you are clothed with the best robe, even the right-eousness of Christ which we wear by faith; when you wear the ring, the signet ring of adoption as a child of God; when your feet are washed and soothed with oil and are now cov-ered with all the woven texture of the Gospel of Peace; then you can give your testimony. You see, you don't need to tell God what He has done for you but the world is waiting to hear what great things the Lord has done for you.

Follow David's example and tell them why you love the Lord. Hear him in Psalm 116. 'I love the Lord because he hath heard my voice and my supplications.' Don't dwell upon your past sins. For heaven's sake, these thoughts can only be entertained in our minds for a moment. And for every such moment let us dwell for an hour upon the Blood of Christ that has washed us and made us clean.

Scripture confirms our need of Faith

Our salvation is linked directly to God's revelation in His Word. Therefore our faith is linked with His Word, the Word of the Lord that is given to us in history, and makes us 'wise unto salvation'. Hear the Scriptures:

> *As the rain cometh down from heaven and*
> *returneth not thither, but watereth the*
> *earth, and maketh it bring forth and that*
> *it may give seed to the sower and bread to*
> *the eater: So shall my word be that goeth*
> *forth out of my mouth: it shall not return*
> *unto me void, but it shall accomplish that*

which I please, and prosper in the thing
whereto I sent it.

(Isaiah 55:11)

Then we have St. Paul writing to the Romans, chapter 10, from verse 8 et seq.

> *The word is nigh thee, even in thy mouth,*
> *and in thy heart: that is the word of faith*
> *which we preach. For there is no differ-*
> *ence between the Jew and the Greek: for*
> *the same Lord overall is rich unto all that*
> *call upon Him. For whosoever shall call*
> *upon the name of the Lord shall be saved.*
> *How then shall they call upon Him in*
> *whom they have not believed?. And how*
> *shall they hear without a preacher?*

Thus we are confirmed in our faith, knowing its genesis in God's elective love is linked to the effectual transmission of His Word to our salvation. Thus our faith is not just subjective. Rather it is linked to the objective revelation of God in history, Christ incarnate, of which the Scriptures testify.

God elects, He does not select. This is an immutable truth. And secondly, we spoke of our need of faith laying hold upon the promises of God, expressing itself in our will. This leads us to the third thought in this trilogy of believing. You see, good beginnings are not enough. Sorrowfully there are those who hear the word with joy for a season. There is an apparent profession of faith. There is an apparent change in the life. Then the enthusiasm fades, the new found love grows cold, the witness loses its conviction. There may not be an overt break with the church, or the fellowship of God's people, but the believer is sluggish, like an over-burdened ship. In extreme cases he is like a ship 'dead in the water'.

Indeed, the name Christian may well be kept up. Many whose love has grown lukewarm long ago, may fill the pews of churches, and yet be estranged from Him who is the Master.

Many become self-sufficient Christians, who travel through the years without feeling the need for a drink from the wells of salvation, or a crumb of the Bread of Life. Anyone who repents and returns to the Lord, must do something more. What is that, you ask?

3

Follow the Lord

Repeatedly in Scripture, believers are called to 'follow the Lord' with the whole heart and mind and strength. When a soul expresses an interest in Christ, immediately he becomes the target for a thousand forces which seek to prevent him becoming an heir of glory. Even as we believe in God and trust in Christ, we are still in the construction stage of our faith. Indeed as long as we are in this world, we are being built up. We are living people, and are spiritually in a process of continual renewal similar to our physical being, where cells are succeeded by cells in a continual process as long as we are alive here on earth.

We must follow the Lord, because we are on the move

There is no rest here. We are pilgrims to Zion, the everlasting city. We cannot idle as we go along. As Malcolm Muggeridge put it, speaking of his Christian journey: 'I have never felt an inclination to linger here.' That, he said, was why John Bunyon's Pilgrim Progress appealed to him.

We must follow the Lord because truth is elusive

Truth is, as it were, always just over the horizon. We get glimpses of truth. But we lose sight of the truth unless we hurry forward. It is like a ship which would like to keep the rim of the sun on the western horizon. Then the ship would always know its position every moment of the day, twenty-four hours a day, until it came to the end of its circumnavigation of the earth. No ship can do that. The captain is thankful to get a sun sight once in twenty four hours. We have one journey and one only from birth to death.

God has called us to follow Christ holding fast to the truth, pressing on towards the mark, keeping Christ before us. If we fall behind or loiter, or divert ourselves with some distraction, we can lose our sense of direction and be out of the Christian race. As St. Paul put it, not all win the prize. Therefore we have to follow, as closely as we can, the Lord who has made the path to glory for us.

We must follow the Lord because time is limited

We have only a limited time. I write this today; tomorrow I may well be in eternity. The believer cannot help thinking like this. 'O Lord, how glorious. I long to enter the portals of the eternal city, to see the Lamb that gives eternal light. I want to be ushered in by your ministering angels, to be taken before the Lord. Unworthy me, give me a place among the multitude of the redeemed, where I may see Him in all His loveliness and all His glory, so that I may feast upon Him for ever and ever.'

Isn't that what heaven is for all who have tasted that the Lord is gracious? So that we must keep as close as we can to the Lord and follow him in every way of earnest discipleship. Though we believe with the heart, we use the mind as the servant of our soul, as a receptive mechanism for truth and ideas. Thus we learn of Christ, applying our minds to His Word.

To follow the Lord means that we SEEK the truth

If you have faith, then you must seek the truth as it is in Christ Jesus, and of which the Scriptures testify. The prophet Hosea made a powerful plea, asking backslidden Israel to return to God. That call is applicable in all ages.

> *Come and let us return unto the Lord: for He hath torn and He will heal us; He hath smitten and He will bind us up. After two days will He revive us in the third day. He will raise us up, and we will live in His sight. Then shall we KNOW if we FOLLOW on to Know the Lord.*

(Hosea 6:1-3)

The word used for FOLLOW means to PURSUE, or to GO AFTER. How reasonable that is. If we believe earnestly, we pursue after truth. We hurry on past all else, seeking Christ who has called us. The desires in our heart, which spring from the urging of our awakened soul, make us FOLLOW Christ as closely as we can.

Sometimes this has a glorious reward that makes all our diligence seems more than worthwhile. At a time when we come up close, Christ turns His face to us. The effect is, we are overwhelmed with joy. Words fail to express the joy within us. We can only bear that experience for a moment, – the Eternal looking at us. But it does happen. Many believers will testify that Christ looked at them, sometimes when circumstances were very dark and their spirits were at a low ebb.

A glimpse of Christ draws us on to follow the Lord

This often keeps believers going, especially when life is hard and they are surrounded by discouragements and a sense of their own unworthiness, and the remembrance of their own sin. But as they pursue after Christ, that momentary sight of the Saviour changes the whole picture to one of love, joy and peace in the Holy Ghost. We literally can suffer all things because we have seen a glimpse of Him. Faith follows Christ closely.

To FOLLOW will mean that we pursue knowledge

It is not enough to learn all kinds of knowledge. We must seek true knowledge, the kind that endures, the kind that goes into the making of God's kingdom, the knowledge of the Lord. This includes all aspects of the Word, the corrective warnings of danger and temptation, the directions for serving God in our generation. Then of course there is all the knowledge of grace and all the promises of God. And who could not dwell on glory and the inheritance of the saints in light? What glorious things new believers have ahead of them! And the whole experience gets better and better as we draw closer and closer to the celestial city. Remember, pursue after Christ, pursue after knowledge. Then, as you are fed with the vitamins of spiritual sustenance, you will go 'from strength to strength,' until you 'appear in Zion at length'.

God's elective love, the need for faith, the need to follow on to know the Lord - keep these thoughts before you and you can't go wrong. You can then use this song. It can be your own song, as you go on to live the Christian life. Remember you are in a great company of people. These thoughts are really just diary notes we share with you, as we move forward with God's people. But they have been tried and proven for the journey to Zion. They rest upon the Covenant of Grace, which in turn seals your destiny from the very beginning, through Elective Love and makes you a member of the Commonwealth of Israel, through the Finished work of Christ.

4

Going Forward

Psalm 126, like the other songs of degrees used in worship at the Hebrew religious festivals, reflects the idea of Progression. Whenever you talk of faith, you talk about people who are on the move. This is easy to understand when we think of Israel. They were a people on the move since Abraham was called by God, out of the land of Ur. As the prototype, if not the genesis, of the Christian Church, we see that same progression as an enduring characteristic of our faith. Here we see in this Psalm, the progression from Babylon, where Israel was in captivity, to Jerusalem.

This return to Jerusalem represented liberation for the Hebrews. They came home from exile, from slavery to freedom, from the emptiness of living in a pagan society, to the richness of living in the context of a Divinely ordered society. From the soulless monotony of living in a society without high goals of spiritual destiny, they had now returned home.

There is nothing like 'coming home'. The emotions that are stirred, the hopes that are awakened, the associations of the past, of one's people, of one's family, flood the mind and heart with a new surge of excitement and life. Foremost among these thoughts for the Hebrews was the transition back to their own land and the holy city of Jerusalem with all the historic associations of God's love to them as the chosen people.

You can understand the euphoric joy of a people starved spiritually for decades, deprived of their spiritual and cultural heritage. The parallel is seen in the emancipation of the states of the Soviet Union and the countries of Eastern Europe which were freed from the chains of communism between 1989 and 1991.

But let's keep our attention on Israel. They were now back in their spiritual homeland, historically permeated with the knowledge of God's revelation and guidance, and inspired with a future based upon God's promises.

You see, the goal of the Land of Promise, which motivated the people to follow Moses out of Egypt and to migrate for forty years in the desert, until they came to Canaan, was not now obsolete. Though they had settled in Canaan for many years since arriving under the leadership of Joshua, they were still a people under the tutelage of God and still the recipients of His promises.

This is a vital aspect of the Hebrews. They were to continue to live in a society of faith, of progression. God had still an abundance of glorious things for them in His plans of mercy and loving kindness. No earthly state, even of the greatest climatic and economic attractiveness,—even a land 'flowing with milk and honey'— could satisfy people, who in the beginning were led to believe in the visionary destiny of a life with Jehovah as Lord. The unseen Jehovah reserves, even for the historic Jews, unseen blessings which have yet to be appropriated. Thus we see the idea of progression.

This Psalm belongs to the ages

It fits the journey of faith in all its varied experiences for people collectively and individually. It fits the change of life through the grace of God, by which believers are delivered continually, from darkness to light, from bondage to freedom, through the indwelling power of Jesus Christ. While some would speak rightly of the judicial act of justification by faith, the experience we seek to express includes an ongoing one of being delivered continually. We are 'plucked as brands from the burning', we are accepted by God; as we bow before the Eternal Son, we are made heirs of glory, and much more. But the journey of faith has to go on, even after the most propitious beginnings, and will be a continuous progression for me and for you as long as we live on earth.

Faith reaching forward to the 'finishing line'

St. Paul put this truth of progression in words for us all, to reflect the continued trust which must be exercised, as faith looks up to God. It also reminds us that our return to God is a life-long experience, where death marks the 'finishing line'. St. Paul uses the word 'to receive fully'. This corresponds to 'follow on to know the Lord', as used by the prophet Hosea, and which must be accepted in the life of one who claims that Christ lives in the heart, and that Christ has set him or her free. Listen to St. Paul: 'Not as though I had already attained, either were already perfect: but I follow after, if that I may apprehend, that for which I am apprehended of Christ' (Philippians 3:12).

There is no room for sitting back or resting on our oars. Faith indeed is a way of life, in which we do not rest but work, in which we do not only reap but plow and sow and nurture and which we not only receive but give.

Our spiritual experience enables us to give out

A life where our faith is continually progressing means that we are growing all the time. We are productive spiritually, and this expresses itself in giving out. Some nights we may go to bed completely emptied, like a cistern which was used all day. But even as the cistern is filled anew by showers of rain, so the believer is filled anew by God. If we live a life of giving out or self-emptying, is that not what Christ did for us? He poured out his soul unto death, holding nothing back. But in that giving, the world has received a living Saviour.

In the eternal union which all believers anticipate with great expectation, the Covenant of Grace will be made so glorious that all the galaxies of the created universe cannot be compared with that gathering, where Christ is the sun, and believers are the myriads of stars that shine for ever and ever.

The community of Praise

When we are born of the spirit, when we are caught in this progression of faith, this giving out of ourselves, then it is natural for us to identify with God's people. Who in this world can compare with them, anyway? Moses could say:

> *'Happy art thou, O Israel: who is like*
> *unto thee, O people saved by the Lord...!*
> (Deuteronomy 33:29)

Is it not also true of the Christian Church in all its diversity, and in its struggles through the centuries? That means we join in the company of praise, singing the songs of Zion, like this Psalm. They become our possession. There are no songs in this world like them. They belong to the ages and indeed it could be that the very psalms that are sung here shall also be sung in glory. I, for one, am convinced that these will be sung in the realms of glory where the redeemed praise the Lamb of God, for ever and ever.

Look at this Psalm, look at the metaphor. The spiritual meaning is boldly evident. 'They that sow in tears, shall reap in joy.' Isn't that sequence true to faith? This is the hope of those who live the life of faith. Follow the metaphor further. 'He that goeth forth and weepeth, bearing precious seed, shall doubtless come again, with rejoicing, bringing his sheaves with him.' What a lovely thought – the progression of faith, a people who are on the move, heirs of glory, with the best yet to come. We no longer set up house here as if for ever, for we live here only for a season. We treat our life as a journey, a succession of days of opportunity to give out, to sow. This affects all we have and all we do and all the time we are given.

This determines our priorities. In principle, we sow the good seed of God's word, the message of His saving grace. We sow it systematically, along with others. We are part of a team. Apart from the loners, and there are disciples who work for Christ independently, the church for the most part, acts in teams. God gives many different gifts and he uses good organizers and administrators to forward the work of the ministry and of evangelism and the continual labour of Christian education and the works of mercy.

Be quite sure, were it not for the influence directly and indirectly of the Christian church in history, there would be little of the developed social services which are taken for granted in secular society. In that vocational occupation of all Christians, engaged and committed to the Master's service, we have the ideal of the Divine Co-operative. When this will be established universally, it will be the fulfilment of the coming of God's Kingdom, 'on earth as it is in heaven.'

In practice this means that we intelligently apply our faith to specific situations in our relations with other people. Reason comes in, common sense is vital, and organization enables all to be done decently and in order. Recalling the farming context of the metaphor, it means using good farming practices, even good technology, so that there is a great sowing, even to the ends of the earth.

The challenge of Christian Sowing

It's nonsense to say that this kind of life is all easy. There are many tears shed on the roadside of the King's Highway. Many hearts are broken. Believers who sow are often despised, and mocked and ridiculed. They are persecuted and slandered. But they go on in the great work to which God has called them, 'casting their bread upon the waters.' Their whole life, personal and vocational, is a sowing. The personal is a 'must', for only as it exists is the vocational stewardship in Christ's name valid. The work of grace never ceases in the believer's life while he is on earth. Therefore he sows, even for himself so that his personal life is fruitful. So that his spiritual experience is a living healthy life where Christ is the guest of guests and always has the best room, the inner chamber of the heart furnished so that it is 'fit for a king', even the king of kings.

As grace flows from heaven, the mind is used as a receiver and monitor to strengthen the spiritual vision.

This is achieved by exposure to all the varied graphic pictures in word and life experience, from the Scriptures and from providence, in the history of the church and its witness.

All this means that the believer is fed and nourished continually in his soul and enabled to sow with spiritual unction and power. This will work wonders for Christ's Cause.

Sowing results in Reaping in God's Time

The prophet set a pattern which coincides in specific terms with the process of returning to the Lord and finding salvation. Listen to Hosea, who illustrates a servant of God, who yearns for people to come to the feast of abundance that God has prepared for those who seek Him:

> *Sow to yourselves in righteousness, reap*
> *in mercy; break up your fallow ground:*
> *for it is time to seek the Lord, till he come*
> *and rain righteousness upon you.*
> (Hosea 10:12)

That sequence is going on all the time, day and night, in every place of human habitation throughout the world. God has his witnesses everywhere. It is the basis of the life of faith that we sow, not knowing when there will be a reaping time but believing that there will be. Blessed are those who sow, but truly doubly blessed are those who sow and also reap. We sow now. Then in God's time, here and in the hereafter, there is the reaping. For many, the harvest of their life is reaped by others, after the sowers are taken to glory. But then, what does it matter?

In the consummation of all things, there will finally be a rerun of history with all the trials and the triumphs of the church, when the great procession of heaven passes the throne of Christ in glory. We are asked here only to be faithful in the sowing. And because we are only little cogs in the great wheels of God's redemptive purposes, we will return 'with sheaves', sharing in the harvest of redemption of Christ's church. And whether the sheaves be small or great, few or many, we will also share in the great rejoicing, with 'joy unspeakable and full of glory'.

Our Personal Perspective

Are you at a standstill? Are you in a rut? Get up, my friend, get going. Listen to the voice of the Spirit of God, calling you, yes, calling you by name. And if you can't hear your name, 'whosever' is the password, so long as you will believe. Mind you, sometimes we are forced to wait. Then we have to wait patiently. God causes many of those He has lined up for his service here and for glory in the hereafter, to wait. It is not uncommon for penitents to be found after a long time on the doorstep of the room of mercy, waiting for the door to open. Words cannot describe the scene as the door opens and Christ takes the returning sinner inside. How can you describe the embrace of redemptive love as Christ puts His arms around the stooping figure, as He covers the shame of his nakedness and washes him and clothes him, to make him a new creation.

Sometimes waiting is a call to redeem the time

Often God prepares us for the future, by giving us some mundane task for the time being. Wherever there is a need, someone has to be used to fill that human need. We may be on the spot at the time. We may have the skills for a particular task which seems far removed from any spiritual calling. Yet the most humble tasks are often vital to the realisation of the great tasks. To see all challenges as important brings a new perspective to all aspects of life.

It also means that waiting is given a deeper meaning, one in which, whatever our hand finds to do, we see it as God's will for us at the time. Our life then becomes a succession of experiences, in which we are continually on the move. Our Christian life is then a progression, and faith translates into a glorious adventure.

One of the greatest discoveries is to find that the Psalms are the outlet of Scripture, providing spiritual nourishment for the believer's journey. This means that we see in the life of faith represented in the Psalms, not only our spiritual needs, but we are also led to corresponding passages in the rest of Scripture which fortify the confidence expressed in the psalms and give our spiritual life the authoritative guidance of the objective revelation of God in history. The full range of the believer's life, right from the beginning of the journey of faith is covered by the Psalms. When was that beginning? That beginning was in God's Elective Love. David was conscious of this. Listen to him, praising God for His omniscience:

> *For Thou has possessed my reins: Thou hast covered me in my mother's womb. I will praise Thee; for I am fearfully and wonderfully made: marvellous are Thy works; and that my soul knoweth right well.*

(Psalm 139:13,14)

Every element in our life contributes to our final victory

Consider a runner, as he crosses the finishing line to victory. The whole race is part of that victory, not just the last minute effort that he makes to win. It may be several circuits round the track before the final sprint. If the race is a marathon, then there are hours of gruelling miles, running over tortuous hilly roads. There is the pouring sweat, the blistered feet, and the exhausting sun.

These are all part of the ultimate victory, as the runner comes at last into the stadium, and makes his final triumphant lap of victory. All that is seen by the crowd is that final approach, with a sustained roar of applause lasting at the most for a minute or two, as the runner sprints to the finishing line.

But that is not the end, in our technologically advanced day. With the camera a video of the whole race from beginning to end can be reviewed, in slow motion. The camera can capture all that went into the victory. It can capture the straining muscles. It can study the dynamic concentration. It can focus in on the single-mindedness, portrayed on the runner's face, as he turns neither to the right nor to the left, in the pursuit of his goal.

What a pattern for the life of the believer! St. Paul saw the similarity, so that he calls the Christians in Corinth to emulate the athletes in self-discipline. 'So run, that ye may obtain' (I Corinthians 9:24).

A Progressive Christian life calls for discipline

Think of the camera again. With it a study can be made of the preparation that went into the effort, for years before the great day of victory. The camera can record the self-discipline, the sacrifice, the abstinence, the moderation, which made the runner, in body and spirit, into a winner. Hear St. Paul again: '...Every man that striveth for the mastery is temperate in all things; Now they do it to obtain a corruptible crown; but we an incorruptible' (I Corinthians 9:25).

The sequence culminates in victory

This is true for the believer in turning to the Lord. The return from bondage to liberty is not something passive even on our part. We become partners with God and in the process of this, we become winners through the grace that works in us. As we reflect upon the believers' pilgrimage, we can see in slow motion the Scriptural elements which comprise the pattern of a victorious and progressive life.

Note a few observations from the Scriptures

They are to be seen as elements of the whole experience. One hesitates to put them in order of importance, for there is diversity in the experience of all believers. But because they are all there, they are ours to possess, and part of the victory.

'Return unto me and I will return unto you'
(Malachi 3:7)

'In returning and rest, shall you be saved'
(Isaiah 30:15)

'I will heal their backslidings. I will love them freely, for mine anger is turned away from him'

(Hosea 14:4)

*'O Israel return unto the Lord, thy God:
for thou hast fallen by thine iniquity.
Take with you words and turn to the
Lord: say unto Him, Take away all iniquity, and receive us graciously: so
will we render the calves of our lips*
(Hosea 14:1,2)

*'I will ransom them from the power of
the grave, I will redeem them from
death: O death I will be thy plagues;
O grave, I will be thy destruction'*
(Hosea 13:14)

These are but a few elements that are in the saving experience of believers. That saving experience could be yours.
Maybe you cannot articulate your experience. You don't
have to. You and I have only to return. The Divine call, the
resolution of will, the forsaking of sin, the reaching forth for
the prize of the high calling in Christ Jesus, the discipline,
the striving, the overcoming— all these are there, not to be
contemplated as a theological exercise, nor to be clinically
examined by the intellect in a cold dispassionate process of
logic. But rather, they are to be assimilated by the whole
person, who is being 'made whole' in that glorious transition from death to life, from sin to salvation, from the power
of darkness to the glorious liberty of the children of God.

In this, Christ makes the lost to be found, the losers are
turned into winners, the condemned are justified, the out-
casts are given a living hope, those sold in bondage are
ransomed, those victims of haunting fears have these replaced
by the incomparable emotions of those who live 'in the love
of God.'

5

Spiritual Freedom

Free to live

When the work of God's grace is realised in our lives, as we return from the captivity of sin to enjoy the glorious liberty of the children of God, then we are really free to live. For the first time we are truly free. There is no power on earth, no spiritual forces of darkness, no demons of the spiritual realms which can touch us. No harm can ever come to us, as long as we live in the Spirit, that unseen wall of love and heavenly power that surrounds the children of God to preserve them from evil. Of course the believer is not free from temptations, and these arise not only from without but from within, because of our innate propensities.

But living or walking 'in the spirit' means that even when we are tempted and tried, God never leaves us without a way of escape. The very exercise of our own will, in the delegated authority that is given to us as God trusts us or puts us in trust for His kingdom, causes us to love Him more, and in the process, we grow, we progress, we get stronger, we mature.

The point is, we are free with the unlimited resources of faith in the unsearchable riches of Christ, to do His will and serve our Lord in our generation.

Free to die

We are not only set free to live, we are also set free to die. Death is viewed very differently by many people. For those who have no hope of life after death, death is the end, the close-down. Life is snuffed out. For those who believe and have eternal life, death is viewed differently. In many ways it is the beginning of great things. Think of all the promises of God. They are to be fulfilled in the hereafter. Death spells the end of all the attendant pain and weaknesses of this life.

That is not to discount the joy and fullness of living on earth. The believer gets a great joy from every sunrise and listening to the little birds as they begin their day with a song of thanksgiving to the Creator. But the fact is there is a time to be born and a time to die. And when the time comes for us to die, no anticipation can match the glorious things that await the children of God, as they pass from the mortal to the immortal.

A place prepared for you

Listen to St. Paul: 'Eye hath not seen, nor ear heard, neither hath entered into the heart of man, the things which God hath prepared for them that love him' (I Corinthians 2:9). You have the assurance that death then, is but the advent of glorious things which are made ready for believers.

Who has made them ready? Yes, our Lord. He comforted his disciples saying, 'In my father's house are many mansions: if it were not so, I would have told you. I go to prepare a place for you' (John 14:2). And there is also this blessing from God. The Holy Spirit reveals what God has prepared for us here in all the blessings of the Gospel. It is often a banquet, a feast for the soul. So that even when all appears lean and desolate, God can provide a feast of good things that rejoices the heart.

Remember the 23rd Psalm. Among all the blessings mentioned here, David tells us in his diary how God prepares a feast of good things in this life. 'Thou preparest a table before me in the presence of mine enemies' (Psalm 23:5).

Death is vanquished

If you are a recipient of saving grace, then death has no pain, no fear. There is no ground for a 'fearful looking to judgement'. You see you are reconciled to God and God is, *ipso facto,* reconciled to you. We can even say with St. Paul, 'For me to live is Christ, and to die is gain' (Philippians 1:21). One of the blessings of the believer's life here is to contemplate the life to come. You do not need to apologize for being carried away in the spirit.

Free to anticipate the future

Being spiritually alive means that you now have a freedom which emancipates you from limitations. You can fill your mind with the gracious promises of God's Word. You let your heart dwell upon them, even the exceeding great and precious promises which have fulfilment in our life here and in the hereafter. Nothing can compare with such experiences of faith, and your whole being gets drawn into the experience, so that a therapeutic current of the spiritual flows right through your whole body.

You smile in disbelief. I tell you this is true, for dwelling upon the glorious things that God has promised, even though we see them only dimly, has a profoundly therapeutic effect upon the whole person. Think of such things that God has prepared for those who are heirs of God and joint heirs with Christ. We just mention a few: the reception in heaven when we reach the end of the race, the banquet, the marriage Supper of the Lamb, believers meeting the King of Peace, sinners saved by grace being 'presented faultless before the presence of His glory', the multitudes of the redeemed singing eternal praise. Then there is the receiving of the 'crown of life', and 'being clothed with immortal robes'.

Surely we are free even to die, for death is vanquished. Hear St. Paul: 'O death, where is thy sting? O grave, where is thy victory?' (I Corinthians 15:55). St. Paul and the prophet Hosea were on the same wavelength. Listen to Hosea:

> *I will ransom them from the power of*
> *the grave; I will redeem them from*
> *death: O death, I will be thy plagues; O*
> *grave, I will be thy destruction.*
> (Hosea 13:14)

We are part of a great multitude which no man can number. Think of all those who have gone on before, since God called man in the Covenant of Grace; think of all those who shall yet believe. It's a glorious theme for the soul to dwell upon, and our relationship with Christ, who is at the right hand of the Father, gives us access into this liberty in which we stand and which is packed with spiritual privileges.

We can only see the Celestial City darkly, but the great thing is that we can see. If you were waiting for a ship to come to your rescue on the ocean, what would it matter if you could see it only dimly. The great thing is that you could see it approaching, getting nearer and nearer.

And that is the way it is in the things God has prepared for them that love him and which become theirs in the here-after. Many believers have come through great tribulations holding on to the promises of God, never letting them go. They have testified that it is these promises, that have kept them from being swept off their feet.

So my friend, as you join believers on the King's Highway that leads to Zion, the everlasting city, even as you glance at those whose choice is the 'pleasures of sin for a season,' strengthen your heart by filling your soul and feasting on the future fulfilment of heavenly joys, in this life and the life to come.

A glance back

Thus the idea of freedom permeates the whole spiritual experience. This is true in depth, as our salvation and the transactions of grace are seen, as it were, in slow motion. Also as we observed in the vital elements of ELECTIVE LOVE, the response of our faith, and the perseverance or following in the steps of the Master, which bring us more and more to know 'him in whom we have believed'.

Christ receives us without reservation

This is the great attractiveness about Christ. There are no conditions. He has paid the purchase of our redemption. His resources are unlimited to remake each one of us, to redeem us from bondage, to set us free, so that no power can reclaim us. We are his, and He is ours for ever. He receives us fully. We are redeemed, we are received, we are understood, we are accepted by Him, in that He has set His love upon us, the dynamic Elective Love of the Covenant of Grace, whereby not one of those who are his possession shall be lost. For He has called us, and saved us, by the washing of His Blood, and the regeneration of the Holy Spirit.

But let us remember, we are dwelling upon the exercise of our faith. That must be our perspective as it takes its course. We see great things, yes, glorious things, sometimes when we are in darkness, for then the Lord God is a light unto us. But however sophisticated and mature our faith may be, yet, as St. Paul humbly acknowledged, we cannot boast that we apprehend or know as God knows.

We reach forth in the life of faith. We are identified and will be till the end, with the broken, the poor, the crippled, the tried. When we think we graduate into a higher class, look out for the warning lights that indicate our very faith and destiny is in jeopardy.

Hear the apostle Paul:

> *'Brethren I count not myself to have apprehended: but this one thing I do, forgetting those things which are behind, and reaching forth unto those things which are before, I press towards the mark for the prize of the high calling of God, in Christ Jesus'*

(Philippians 3:13-14)

And whatever progress we make in spiritual knowledge and experience, it is all ascribed to the grace of God, even as the

Psalmist David says on behalf of Israel: 'When the Lord turned again the captivity of Zion.'

The eyes of the world are always watching the righteous

I think there is a kind of secret longing, a kind of envy of those who have put their hope and confidence in the living God. When we read Psalm 126, we note that not only were God's people full of joy at what the Lord had done for them, but also we are told that the heathen also took note and talked among themselves, saying, 'The Lord hath done great things for them.'

6

God's Promise

Always, in the pleadings of the Scriptures, God not only calls the church to return to Him, but God Himself promises to return to the church. God has a special love for His church. This is seen in the Old Testament. Hear the incomparable assurance given through the prophet Zechariah, that God loves to dwell in Israel and in the Christianised Israel of the New Testament church, extending to the future multitudes.

> *Sing and rejoice, O daughter of Zion:*
> *for lo I come, and I will dwell in the*
> *midst of thee, saith the Lord. And many*
> *nations shall be joined to the Lord in*
> *that day, and shall be my people: and I*
> *will dwell in the midst of thee...*
>
> (Zechariah 2:10,11)

Jesus told his disciples that the church extended to the gathering of little numbers of believers who share their faith in believing witness and worship.

> *'Again I say unto you, ...where two or three*
> *are gathered together in my name, there*
> *am I in the midst of them'*
>
> (Matthew 2:19,20)

God is always in His church

God is always working somewhere in this world, through the dynamic presence of the Holy Spirit. He withdraws from the church where His name is dishonoured and His Word is scorned. It is impossible for the whole church across the globe to be in bondage to sin at any one time, for God has promised that He will always have His witnesses in every age and in every place. But where there is the bondage of sin, then God, and the liberty and joy of His presence are not to be found.

There can be no joy where the Holy Spirit withdraws the work of His immediate presence. Pity the poor people who have a form of religion without the glorious life of the Holy Spirit, which brings the Power of God into life and worship through the acknowledgement of God's Holy Word.

This is the root cause of the many maladies of our sophisticated age, making a tragic connection between Divine withdrawal and the depression and oppression of the human spirit.

A reason for laughter

Laughter makes the world go round— that is, true laughter, not the hysteria of mockery or cheap humour. When Israel saw what God had done for them, their 'mouths were filled with laughter, and their tongue with melody'. What therapy for the human spirit, dwelling upon the wonderful works of God in the human life. What incomparable humour, such glorious things being done for us by God, that are beyond our 'wildest dreams'.

This therapeutic humour was linked to the sequence that took place. We are told that the people who came back, in the successive returns, with Zerubbabel, and then with Nehemiah, had little or no knowledge of God's holy Word, just as millions of those in Communist-dominated Eastern Europe professed that they had unlearned their Christian heritage under the communist regime.

When Ezra the scribe found the Book of the Law and opened the scrolls, and read out God's Word, many people wept. Old folks wept because they remembered the days of long ago when they had worshipped as children, before being taken captive; younger people and middle-aged people wept, because they realised, as they heard the Word, just what they had been deprived of, over all these years, even the glorious and precious promises revealed to them. For truly, 'man cannot live by bread alone, but by every word which proceedeth out of the mouth of God' (Matthew 4:4).

Christ's Second Coming is God's Return in full

God's presence in the church on earth is something like the ebb and flow of the tides round the coast. And as well, there are the bi-annual periods of the equinox, when there are particularly high tides. Just think of it, when Christ will come, what a glorious full tide of God's presence there will be. There is a case for believing that when the church returns to the Lord in a great awakening, it will be as if different streams of church life across the world will rise and join to become a mighty river. When this takes place in personal and corporate repentance, it will fulfil the conditions in which Christ shall return in a glorious visitation, that will bring rejoicing to the church. This return to God must comprise all the parts of the universal church. Only as all segments of the church join in unison to weep for sin, and to will for Christ's presence, will we have grounds for seeing Christ's return. But ultimately, only the Father knows the times and the seasons for all the events that are prophesied and promised. 'And he (Jesus) said unto them, it is not for you to know the times or the seasons, which the father hath put in His own power' (Acts 1:7).

The role of the Jews

We can not be certain, but the general tenor of Scripture suggests that the Jews, the historic prototype of God's people, will be in the van of this return. God is the God of history. The church cannot be separated from history, nor divest itself of its history, good and bad as that history may be. The spirituality of the church in the presence of God in Christ by the Spirit, or in the fullness of Christ's return, is linked with the earth, and man's corporate journey to the everlasting Zion, the city of God.

God calls his church to return. Yes, He calls the world, in the call of the Gospel. The effectual calling is expressed in actuality, by those that do return, and comprises all the separate parts or fellowships which we call the Christian church, in all its diversity.

Christ's prayer for unity

As a rule we do not look for authoritative doctrine in the Psalms. At the same time they reflect the doctrines that are contained in the Scriptures. There is a reciprocal effect as we relate the Psalms to the rest of Scripture. We take what Christ said or implied as authoritative. Thus when He prayed in the Garden of Gethsemene, we cannot but get the message of His will that the church may dwell in unity. And the prayer that He made embraced the whole of the church which should believe in all the ages to come.

Hear Him:

> *Neither pray I for these alone, but for them also that shall believe on me, through their word. That they all may be one, as Thou Father art in me, and I in Thee, that they also might be one in us; that the world may believe that Thou hast sent me.* (John 17:20,21)

St. Paul says, 'So we being many are one body in Christ' (Romans 12:5).

Go back to Isaiah: 'They shall see eye to eye, when the Lord shall bring again Zion' (Isalah 52:8).

Then we have Psalm 133, with the theme of unity, 'Behold how good and how pleasant, it is for brethren to dwell together in unity.'

Unity is often confused with unanimity

The great thing about the unity of the church of Christ is that it is full of diversity. But it is still one body and one spirit and one essential core of belief. God calls the church to unity of the spirit, but God doesn't expect all believers to be unanimous on all the views and interpretations of the application of Scripture.

Man and his environment produce diversity. Sometimes that diversity is very reasonable. For instance, when the church in one time, placed undue emphasis on one point of truth to the exclusion of another, then you had a reaction, and possibly an exaggerated one, in order to counteract what appeared to be an imbalance.

We will only say that there is a healthy unity of spiritual affinity among believing Christians, that does not require a vote of unanimity. There is already a unity of the spirit in the diversity that obtains and will always obtain as in other areas of human life. We are not clones of one believer. Christians are not 'Yes' men, coming out of a mold.

Indeed believers are the very ones that do not go along with the tide. By their renewed nature, they tend to think and exercise the freedom which God has given them in Christ, but always in the context of brotherly love, even to those who are not believers. A little difference of emphasis on a particular doctrine, or the presence of conflict in a nation, can, as history is witness, cause one segment of the church there to be very different in its characteristics from those of the remainder.

The trend towards unity

If we take a balanced view of Scripture, there ought to be a general trend towards unity. There are great blessings in practising unity in fellowship and worship and in service. Wherever believers are the children of light, in a world of darkness and evil, there should be fellowship, even with those that see differently, yet are also the children of light. Indeed, the very fact that we can have fellowship with those with whom we differ, yet are in Christ's church, is evidence that we are the children of light. For it requires grace to acknowledge the sincerity of those with whom we disagree on some points.

Hear John: 'If we walk in the light, as He is in the light, we have fellowship, one with another' (I John 1:7).

God wants the church to be united. This unity is linked to His return in Christ. 'There shall be one fold, and one shepherd' (John 10:16).

And St. Paul asserts, 'So we being many, are one body in Christ' (Romans 12:5).

God's Power is a unifying influence

The prince of the powers of darkness wants to divide people, to sow dissension. He follows the maxim, 'divide and conquer', the well known political tactic of those who seek partisan power. The way of Christ is different. It draws people together. The power of the love of God dissolves animosities. It overlooks differences, and brings in a new kind of humanity in our relations with one others.

God's church is synonymous with history

God's church is identifiable as that movement in history which dynamically works to bring in righteousness and fulfil the claims of Christ to the earth as His possession. God has promised the earth and its peoples to the Eternal Son. (Ps.2, 7-8). This is a divine decree given in the Psalms, reflecting the doctrinal assertion that 'the earth is the Lord's and the fullness thereof' (I Corinthians 10:26).

Protest is a healthy ongoing process

When we look at the history of the church, we see fragmentation. This is seen in the split in the Middle Ages between the East and West, now the Catholic and the Orthodox. It is seen again in the Reformation in the 16th century. But these are but collective terms which cover thousands of protest movements at one time or another. Indeed this is an ongoing process of protest, which signifies spiritual health in the universal church. There is a corollary to this fragmentation. From time to time the separate parts coalesce or come together, as a rule in different groupings.

Dr. Thomas Chalmers, the Disruption leader of the Free Church in Scotland, stated this as a principle when he led half of the church in Scotland out of the establishment. 'We leave a vitiated establishment; we will return to a pure one,' he said. In practice this is realised in a modified way. The fact is that sometimes when there is a return or reunion, new liberalisations of doctrine are introduced. The result is that there is always a segment whose love for the 'tried ways' of the old makes it impossible for them to stomach what they see as the diluted doctrines of the new.

Separation brings its own penalties

Since there is no life without continual change, separation even in the defence of one principle can provide the atmosphere for negative witness and ingrown perspectives. There will always be the need in the church for reformers. And when these are not heeded, there will always be the justification for healthy walk-outs in the church. But there should also be a continual returning. Otherwise this healthy process is impossible. There must be this impulse to return, to come together.

No separate group was born in a vacuum. Rather, as St. Paul said, we are debtors to all. But especially to the church of history, call it catholic or universal. We are debtors to the monks who kept the lamps of the sancturay alight in the monasteries, during the plunderings of Northern Europe by the Vikings. We are debtors to the Eastern churches who preserved the New Testament teachings in the manuscripts stored in the libraries of Constantinople and rediscovered in the West, thus producing the Renaissance. There must be this impulse to come together. If not, too often separation leads to the doctrine of Separatism, an ecclesiastical form of class distinction.

You see, we may claim that 'God rules with us'. That may be our claim. But the test of being the true Israel is, whether or not 'we rule with God'. For that is the meaning of ISRAEL. Our claim may be so vehement and assertive that we lose sight of this mandatory requirement.

If the latter obtains, it implies that we submit to God's government in the world, which was given to Christ and of which the church in its historic continuity, with all its faults, is witness and executive.

The presence of the Lord requires continual prayer

The lines between heaven and believers are engaged night and day. Worship, adoration, thanksgiving rise to the throne of God. And there are all the supplications for mercy, the pleas for forgiveness, the cries of distress, the calls for reassurance. Then there are the emergency calls from those who have fallen, the S.O.S. messages from those who are in the midst of a storm, the requests for bearings from those who are like ships lost in fog, who are spiritually disorientated, and have become captive to the fears of their imagination.

This continual prayer is a collective intercession for God to deliver the church from bondage, to continually set it free. For it is true that the church is restricted. It is oppressed. It is reasonable that it prays night and day through the ages for the Lord to return in the fullness of His power and the joy of His presence.

The prayer of the church and the prayer of Creation

Hear St. Paul: 'For the earnest expectation of the creature waiteth for the manifestation of the Sons of God' (Romans 8:19). And in the same chapter; ' For we know that the whole creation groaneth and travaileth in pain together until now' (Romans 8:22).

The church cries like the returned exiles from Babylon, who, even as they rejoiced in their return, yet continued to seek totality, in the fullness of God's return to them. 'Turn again our captivity O Lord, as the streams in the south' (verse 4).

The church is dependent upon God for His grace

The need for continual grace causes the church in the community of all true believers, to be dependent upon God. It means that the church is humbled by its own inadequacy. But by the same token, because all authority is given to Christ to bring the church out of the wilderness of this world to glory, the church lives continually by daily drawing upon the grace of God. That grace is not given automatically.

People have to seek the Lord early, to go out together like Israel on their desert journey, rising early every day to receive the manna God had provided for them. And although a pilgrim started his journey of faith a hundred years ago, and is still alive on earth, he or she lives on this premise, spiritually as well as physically, 'Give us this day our daily bread'. All who have once tasted that the Lord is gracious will be found in the supermarket of the Psalms, shopping for their spiritual needs.

7

Coming Home

St. Luke tells us that when Christ gave the assurance of his continued presence, the disciples 'returned to Jerusalem with great joy' (St. Luke 24:53). The joy is not a spurious sentiment. It arises in the hearts of believers as their expectations of great and mighty things take the place of despair and the petty goals that absorb our attention when our eyes are on the seen rather than the unseen.

We see in Psalm 126 this joy expressed in the historical setting of the exiled Jews coming back to Jerusalem. This returning was not a once and for all event, but part of a continuous process. As we dwell upon the psalm and identify it with the particular event, the pathos, the emotions, the overwhelming effect of the occasion, serve to illustrate the recurring joy which always accompanies the returning of people, collectively as the church, or as individuals, in a saving experience of grace.

Thus we see the event where a large number of exiles return under the joint direction and leadership, both civil and ecclesiastical, of Nehemiah, and Ezra respectively.

There is a dramatic setting as the people are directed to observe the historic Feast of Tabernacles. When we remember all the connotations of the history of Israel as God led them forth out of bondage in Egypt and their subsequent journey for forty years in the desert, living in tents, we can only assume that the human emotions of nostalgia and generic association must have made this a landmark occasion of intensive joy. But over and above that, the focus of attention is directly concentrated upon the rediscovery of the Book of the Law, or the first Five Books of Moses, in God's House, and the reading of it to the people.

> *And Ezra opened the book in the sight*
> *of all the people; (for he was above all*
> *the people;) and when he opened it, all*
> *the people stood up. ... So they, (the*
> *leaders and teachers who read) caused*
> *the people to understand the Law......So*
> *they read in the book of the Law of God*
> *distinctly, and gave the sense, and*
> *caused them to understand the reading.*
> *And Nehemiah.... and Ezra, and the*
> *Levites that taught the people said unto*
> *all the people, This day is holy unto the*
> *Lord your God; mourn not nor weep.*
> *For all the people wept when they heard*
> *the words of the law; Then he said unto*
> *them, Go your way, eat the fat, and drink*
> *the sweet, and send portions unto them*
> *for whom nothing is prepared: for this*
> *day is holy unto our Lord: neither be ye*
> *sorry; for the joy of the Lord is your*
> *strength.*   (Nehemiah 8:5-10)

Rediscovering the essence of God's historic message for man, in his Word, brings an exultant joy. The experience is exquisite. It is like a 'dream come true'. In the Psalm it is said, the people could hardly believe what they heard, but it was in the sense that it seemed 'too good to be true'. The song expresses it thus, 'We were like dreamers,' as their hearts were filled with a great and incomparable joy. They shouted for joy, so that their voices joined in glorious cadences of melody rising like incense to heaven, for God was speaking to them through His Law, the message of His everlasting and redeeming love.

They were filled with melody. Joy is the melody of the soul. The soul sings when it is set free. Here is true joy. And wherever souls find the Lord, in a penitent return, as they meet the Saviour who, like a shepherd, is out seeking the lost, you have this music of joy. Of course, only in eternity will it be full in the fulfilment of God's promises to His church. Then the capacity of the soul will be far greater, but even now on earth our souls can be full of joy. Jesus said, 'These things have I spoken unto you, that my joy might remain in you, and that your joy might be full' (John 15:11).

The joy we experience on earth in believing is generically the same as that which fills the redeemed in glory. Even as the raindrop is really part of the cycle of precipitation, and therefore part of the ocean, so the joy that fills the soul is part of that ocean of eternal joy that will fill the church with the swelling volume of dynamic praise, and will cause the whole earth to give glory to the King Eternal, Jesus Christ our Lord.

We see that this joy is transcendent

This joy is transcendent because there are longings latent in exiles, which at last are awakened and met by liberation. And those who live without returning to God, are exiles. They are far from home, their eternal home and the love of their heavenly Father. The price of their fare home is already paid for on Calvary, with the Blood of Christ.

All that is required is for you, if this is your case, to put a call through to God. At one time you had to go to a phone to make a call in the telephone system. Now, people can phone from their car or from any place where they may be.

How true of God's communication system for souls to return to His redemptive love! The heavenly cellular phone system has always been there, so that all you need is to call upon God with a plea for His mercy. And lo, in a moment, you will be the subject of His grace, for God is never far from any one of us. And if you were unaware before of latent longings in your soul, you will now have such longings that 'none but Christ will satisfy'.

This joy is transcendent because there is a perpetual prayer rising from the hearts of the devout in all ages, for a great return of the church. All people who dwell on earth, in all continents, and of all ethnic and cultural backgrounds, are potentially identified with this people.

This is a people 'made willing' in a day of God's power, so that they justify being called the Israel of God, for they are a people who 'rule with God'.

This joy is transcendent because captivity or allegiance to any power, except that of God, brings humiliation. The freedoms relating to the Hebrew God-given heritage did not obtain in an alien land. Nor do the freedoms relating to the Christian life obtain, when believers live in any relationship of corporate community or personal life-style which is outwith the rule of the church of Christ.

There were people in Israel then, and God will always have them in every age, one of the choicest minorities, who had the burden of the world's good on their hearts. Their conviction is that the world will never know any semblance to a Utopian fulfilment without a great return to God and the church of Jesus Christ. Simeon belonged to that minority.

He is known to us as the one who saw Jesus as the fulfilment of the Jewish Messianic hope (Luke 2:25). He had a vision of a restored Israel, a people who 'rule with God' in the 'law of Christ', and who chose to believe in Zion when it seems forsaken. Today as the third millennium rises over the horizon of history, what a glorious beginning if we should see a sunrise where the rays of the sun of righteousness would reach out to herald a new day across the earth.

This joy is found in worship

Worship demands acknowledgement of the one living and true God. We observe this in the context of Israel's return to Jerusalem from exile. We read that they worshipped the Lord. We read how reforms were brought in, how the house of the Lord was rebuilt from the ruins, how the people listened to the preaching of the Word of God, and how this was applied sometimes very painfully, to their own lives and their society. God made his presence felt among them. This arose from finding again God's covenant promises. When the scrolls of the Pentateuch – the five books of Moses – were found, and when Ezra read out from them in the hearing of the people, we are told there was such a reaction that it remains the graphic illustration of what potentially happens when ever a person or a people give attentive ear to the preaching of the Gospel. We are told that 'many wept... many shouted for joy' (Ezra 3:12).

What a day that was, the like of which had never been known during the lost long years by the rivers of Babylon. And the prevailing image that is projected is the worship, the adoration, the praise of the living God. You see, they heard how He was their God, Jehovah, and how they were really His people. This worship was not the hysteria of a moment, an hour spent in a big hall, or football stadium, though the arresting preaching of an evangelist, is for amny of God's people, the turning point of their lives. This worship, born in tears of true penitence and joy, took the form of order and reverence and beauty, the beauty of holiness.

Listen to the reporter, Ezra, as he records the picture of worship on the great day when the foundation of the rebuilt temple was laid:

> *And they sang together by course, in praising and giving thanks unto the Lord; because he is good, for his mercy endureth forever. And all the people shouted with a great shout when they praised the Lord...But many of them priests and the Levites and chief of the fathers, who were ancient men, that had seen the first house, when the foundation of this house was laid before their eyes, wept with a loud voice; and many shouted aloud for joy. So that the people could not discern the noise of the shout of joy from the noise of the weeping of the people: for the people shouted with a loud shout, and the noise was heard afar off.* (Ezra 3:11-13)

I am sure that Psalm 95 expresses the articulate worship of the people that day. And it still does the same in the worship of people who 'come home' to God in the third millennium.

O come let us sing to the Lord: let us make a joyful noise to the rock of our salvation. Let us come before his presence with thanksgiving, and make a joyful noise unto him with psalms. For the Lord is a great God, and a great God above all gods.come, let us worship and bow down: let us kneel before the Lord our maker. For he is our God; and we are the people of his pasture, and the sheep of his hand.

(Psalm 95:1-7)

The whole return of the Hebrews, in spite of much opposition, became the talking point over the known world of that day. Listen to the prophet and journalist, Nehemiah, recording the news item: 'God had made them to rejoice with great joy. The joy of Jerusalem was heard even afar' (Nehemiah 12:3). And in the psalm before us we read: 'then said they among the heathen, The Lord hath done great things for them.'

The joy of the people was exultant

And the joy of all who return to the Lord is always exultant. Especially is this true where there is a great awakening and corporate return, with all the implications of dynamic service that follow for the glory of God and the good of the whole community round about. Wherever there is revival of true religion, there are great benefits that spill over into the whole community, in a quickened conscience in commerce, and a return to high standards in conduct and relationships with other people. The joy of living under the canopy of our 'heavenly Father's love' is an exultant joy.

It's there in every age, where sinners, backsliders, prodigals like you and me, return to the fold, and find the Father waiting to be gracious. You see, believers prove that joy, like those Hebrews long ago who returned from captivity in Chaldea or what we call Iraq, to their real home, where God had chosen to dwell with his people. Exultant joy accompanies the triumph of faith over all powers within ourselves and without, which would weaken us and steal our heritage from us.

What we see in the case of the Jews in Psalm 126 and amplified in the records of Scripture, is a victory celebration. If you looked and saw how much there was yet to be done, to rebuild again the ruined house of God and the ancient city of peace, you might well wonder what there was to sing about. If you examined the people's religious knowledge, and found how lacking this was in most, you might not be aware of the unseen, the unsearchable riches of God, the great resources, from which God is able and willing to supply all the believers' needs, to make new people, and a new world.

Even as their enemies take flight, the people, then and now, break forth into praise. They are of one accord. Their worship reaches heaven, even to the throne of the triune God. And in that worship is expressed the incomparable joy, which exceeds all expectations.

8

Learning True Joy

The key to this supreme and exultant joy is often found through a bitter experience. Desires and longings arise in the heart. You begin to reflect upon your life. Even as you taste the bitterness of sin, you cannot but recall the Biblical teaching, the lessons of early life, the gracious life of the godly, the love and concern of parents, the peace and happiness of a good home. For most of the younger generation of the Hebrews, and most of the younger generation of people today, there is often little to remember, and often that which is remembered has been psychologically perverted by hostility to Christ and all that is good regarding family and home and religion.

That is a major reason why there is spiritual emptiness on a large scale, in nations who have used up their spiritual capital, and are bankrupt and in debt spiritually and morally. But think of the positive. When desire and longing at last lead to decisive action and we leave the 'far city' to return home, God makes clear his mighty power is there to deliver us. There were many lessons learned by God's people in Babylon, in the country we call Iraq today. The people learned 'the hard way'. And likewise, many lessons are learned in all ages, 'the hard way', by those who are effectually called and chosen for glory. Among these lessons is this, that joy, true joy, is found alone in God. The parable of the sower, which Jesus gave the church, is still true. And there is much of that parable in the song these people sang long ago. 'Those who sow in tears, shall reap with joy. He that goeth forth, and weepeth, bearing precious seed, shall doubtless come again, with rejoicing, bearing his sheaves with him.'

If you look at the book of the prophet Hosea, you will see that the process of coming back, of people returning to God, and God returning to people, is seen again and again. The name for such experiences include times of revival, times of renewal, times of refreshing, times of reformation. Wherever the sun rises and sets on the earth this process is going on, in an unending work of the Spirit. There are sudden and spectacular events, when revival flares up like a great light on the horizon. On the other hand apart from such glorious moments, there are many exiles 'returning home' where they belong, to their spiritual destiny in Christ's church and with Christ's people. There is no fanfare, there are no news flashes, there are no newspaper headlines, but there must be at any one time, a great number of people from all walks of life, and from all kinds of circumstances, in the process of returning home to God and finding the secret of true and lasting joy. They come from the north and the south and the east and the west and they shall be gathered at last together to sit down at the heavenly table, in the habitations of glory. My friend, God is near to everyone of us (Acts 17:22). Make a call. Let it be a cry from the heart, let it be an S.O.S. for the rescue mission of his redeeming love, designed especially for those who want to 'come home' and find true joy.

It is God's elective love that initiates the process of coming home. When he sets his love on you, then a process of spiritual activity takes place which culminates in exultant and exquisite joy. In this spiritual activity, we can identify at least four factors that inter-relate. These are remembrance, reverence, instruction, spiritual-mindedness.

Remembrance produces reflection. The mind starts thinking. The word of God in one way or another impinges upon the person's thoughts. A new attitude becomes manifest, even like the children of Israel who now reflected upon their relationship to their Creator and their God. This was a new dimension for them. They began to thlnk of the source of life, the real power that sustained the earth, and human society. Not only so but they came to realise that that same Creator was the God of history, and specifically of their history, as God's chosen people. They had been surrounded by a humanist culture which had fed on its own gods, in sport, in government and culture. There was a coterie of 'intellectuals' who, like the Pharisees of Jesus' day, were entrenched in power over people, promulgating transient ideas and theories of a day, as if these were the last word of truth.

Now for the first time, these people realised that behind the apparent, there was the real. Behind the technology of aqueducts, behind the sciences that produced the dazzling wonders of the famous 'hanging gardens' of Babylon, behind the intellectual grasp of knowledge, there was God, the source of all power, and wisdom and might, the creator of the ends of the earth'. And when there is this realisation, by any people in any age, it introduces them to a new dimension, even the idea of holiness. 'For without holiness, no man shall see God' (Hebrews 12:14). This new self-awareness, as if one is suddenly alone before the living God, the ultimate and absolute, brings in a new attitude, one of humble reverence, or 'fear of the Lord'. The relationship between God and his people is one in which there is the consciousness of God's holiness. God is far above his creatures, as the potter who shapes the clay into different vessels of usefulness and beauty is above the works of his hands. The reverence or 'fear of the Lord' must not be derived from the knowledge or 'insights' of man, however erudite the latter may be. Nor can it derive from the 'counsels of men' in church or state. The reverence is, as it were, induced by coming face to face with God in His presence. The Hebrews had this as the fundamental basis of their faith. It is seen again and again in the experience of Abraham, Moses, the prophets and many others, including the psalmist, David. This reverence and awe leads to a new perspective, a basis for a new and profitable and joyous partnership with God, where his presence, his power, his wisdom, his will, his word are uniquely recognized for faith and life.

We will quote from Isaiah, who makes the distinction between the religion that is built upon the wisdom of men, and that which is built upon God's revelation and wisdom.

> *Wherefore the Lord said, Forasmuch as this people draw near me with their mouth, and with their lips do honour me, but have removed their heart far from me, and THEIR FEAR TOWARD ME IS TAUGHT BY THE PRECEPTS OF MEN: Therefore, behold, I will proceed to do a marvellous work among this people, even a marvellous work and a wonder: for the wisdom of their wise men shall perish, and the understanding of their prudent men shall be hid.*
> (Isaiah 29:13,14)

The reflection upon life leads to reverence, the true kind, 'the fear of the Lord' which is the beginning of wisdom.

The assertion of man as the source of knowledge or the arbiter of truth, is like 'putting the cart before the horse'. God says:

> *Surely your turning of things upside*
> *down shall be esteemed as the potter's*
> *clay, for shall the work say of him that*
> *made it, He made me not, or shall the*
> *thing framed say of him that framed it,*
> *He had no understanding?*

(Isaiah 29:16)

Let us think, rather, of the change that took place in this people and takes place in all who come to know this exultant joy. Isaiah never forgets that true religion is one of joy.

Listen to him.

> *The meek also shall increase their joy in*
> *the Lord, and the poor among men shall*
> *rejoice in the Holy One of Israel.*

(Isaiah 29:19)

Here the preacher or teacher comes in, one who is a skilled workman in the use of the word. The word of God is shown to be 'the only rule to direct us, how we may glorify and enjoy Him' (The Westminster Shorter Catechism). After the receptiveness to teaching from the doctrines of the Word, you have spiritual-mindedness. This is none other than the work of the Holy Spirit melting the heart, rousing the soul, losing the hardness, dissolving the corrosion. Then you have the Spirit taking the things of Christ, in all the efficacy of the atoning Blood, and sealing the will to God's saving purpose. In this, the soul and Christ are knit together in the Covenant of Grace. The union is sealed with the love of

Christ, which 'passeth knowledge'. If this is your experience, you are free, you are liberated. You are free to live, you are free to die, and yet to live forever. This is the key to 'joy unspeakable and full of glory'. And the key to that glorious exultant experience which floods the whole being with exquisite and everlasting joy, is spelt out by remembrance, by reverence, by doctrinal instruction, by spiritual-mindedness.

9

Liberation

The common denominator of all true spiritual movements is liberation, emancipation, release. The chains of addiction, the fetters of fear, the slavish pressures of peer or the tinsel pull of popularity, give way as the soul breaks out of slavery.

No wonder you now feel like singing. And you can join in singing this song of liberation, with the exiled people of God in the ever present 'gathering' of Christ's sheep throughout history. Take a glance at Israel's situation while they were still in Babylon. They wept with self-pity and misery at their circumstances, as they sat on the river bank. You see, the older ones had memories of Zion and the joyous blessings of Jerusalem, and the younger generations were told about their heritage, and were taught in their homes the fundamentals of their national faith. But though they knew about their religion of joy, the practice of it, collectively, was proscribed, for they were a subject people. Indeed they were made fun of, their captors taunting and mocking them, and making a jest of their religion. Listen to the record of these miserable times:

> *By the rivers of Babylon, there we sat down yea we wept when we remembered Zion. We hanged our harps upon the willows in the midst thereof. For there they that carried us away captive required of us a song; and they that wasted*

us, required of us mirth, saying, Sing us
one of the songs of Zion. How shall we
sing the Lord's song in a strange land?
(Psalm 137:1-4)

Now it was a different story altogether. Israel could sing the Lord's song, not man's song. They were free, they were liberated, they were saved. And all who return to God through his Crucified and Risen Son, Jesus Christ, are free, are liberated, are saved. They are called to join in, singing the Lord's songs. And these are not the songs of men, but the songs and spiritual hymns, which God has given his church, even the Book of Psalms, as primary for universal worship. Cultivate a love for the Psalms, and you will never rest without them. And if you sing them here on earth, I cannot but believe that they will comprise the singing material of heaven.

Let the church everywhere return. Then all people that dwell on earth can sing. It's no use to sing while still in bondage to sin and committed to 'the world'. Like Israel in Babylon, you can only sing a mournful dirge.

When people are liberated by the power of God, they sing a song of coming back where they belong; they sing a song of coming home; they sing a song of abundance; they sing a song of worship and thanksgiving, at the cross of Jesus Christ; they sing a song of discovery of the liberating law of God. God puts his spirit upon them and writes it in their hearts.

Jeremiah the prophet declares what God does for Jew and Gentile, when they come back to him through the atoning work of Christ:

> *But this shall be the covenant that I will*
> *make with the house of Israel; After*
> *those days, saith the Lord, I will put my*
> *law in their inward parts, and write it*
> *in their hearts; and will be their God,*
> *and they shall be my people.*
>
> (Jeremiah 31:33)

This transformation gives us a new life altogether. Thus you have a song of rediscovery of God's law, the word of his love, and in Christ the law is seen as the channel of God's love. Thus the praise rises to heaven's throne in an expression of obedience to God's law, of service in the church of Christ, and of faith in His redeeming grace.

This is a song of assured joy

Of course we can only taste the joy of the Lord here. But even a taste that God is good satisfies the soul. All kinds of limitations require us to feed on Christ and to drink of the living waters each day. The joy is assured, but in a curious way it is sustained within us by the hunger and thirst for righteousness that brings us continually to the feet of Christ. You see what this means. The more we hunger and thirst after righteousness, the greater the joy within us, as our hearts are filled. And when our hearts are full, our consciousness is pervaded with the fragrance of the Saviour, the 'altogether lovely one', and now and then, we may glimpse the Saviour's face. I say, now and then, yes, even though it be once in our life journey here, the joy of seeing that face can never be taken from us. Then our capacity to receive the fullness of Christ's joy will be like a full tide coming in, when our souls are emancipated from the flesh, and we are brought into the eternal banqueting house of God's love.

There is no escapism in this. Rather, this leads to our reaching out, to a vigorous faith, to dynamic service in Christ's name. It leads to the forsaking of many things, which are not evil or bad in themselves, but which have to give way to the pursuit of God-given goals. For to those who return to God, and to whom God has returned, Christ is the Lord, he is the master, his command is their will. But he also is the source of power to give up all else that would hinder. If you or I have found the joy of the Lord, then let us 'count it all joy' as we cast our bread upon the waters, for it shall surely return after many days.

While it is true to say that there is a strong affinity between all people on earth, we are not arbiters of other people's destiny. We are reminded that there are 'first which shall be last and last which shall be first'. Indeed, we should remember that the ultimate judgement of every one of us is in God's hands. There are many millions, who at a given moment seem to belong to the world, but only God knows in his foreknowledge and foreordaining will, those that shall be the 'whosoever wills'. In a general sense, there is great unhappiness and dissatisfaction in the world. There is also sadness and the shadow of despair. Behind the mask of superficial peace, there is the joyless soul, the heart that never knows the therapy of overflowing with the fullness of Divine love, the mind that is a stranger to the peace eternal. For 'God will keep him in perfect peace, whose mind is stayed on him' (Isaiah 26:3).

In the light of this, in a strange way, there is rejoicing in the world when God visits his church in a special return and outpouring of the Holy Spirit. There is a deep hunger among all people on earth for spiritual fulfilment. When joy is rumoured to be in the church, when people are filled with laughter, when they speak out and say it is like ' a dream come true', many so-called outsiders sit up and take notice. They wonder what is going on. What have these Christians found? When believers experience the 'joy of the Lord', the church is awakened with a new dynamic.

Believers just cannot keep quiet. To have that joy and keep it to oneself is out of the question. The nature of knowing the joy of the Lord is linked to the will of God for the world. There is a natural curiosity on the part of the outsiders who ask, 'Why are these Christians so full of joy?'

10

The Church's Purpose

In the 1880s, news of the great gold discovery in the Yukon, in Northern Canada, spread south and reached San Fransisco. Almost overnight all the crews of the big ocean sailing ships signed off the ships, and headed north to the Yukon in search of their dream of riches. Alas, for only a small fraction of these would the dream become a reality.

In like manner many are drawn by the witness of the church's joy, to come themselves to the fountain of all joy, but with this difference, that all who respond receive the riches of Christ. This is a glorious role for the church to fulfil in the world. It is meant to be like a beacon of light, like a city set on a hill. Jesus reminded his disciples that their witness had the purpose of attracting strangers to the Gospel.

'Let your light so shine before men, that they may see your good works, and glorify your Father which is in heaven' (Matthew 5:16). Shining is a positive, uplifting, enlightening process. We ask God to shine on us with the light of his countenance. There is one word among others in the Hebrew language used for shining whose literal meaning is, 'to cause to rejoice'. It is used only once in Scripture, in Psalm 104. But what a glorious usage. What a role for Christians on the stage of this world, to cause others to rejoice. This is part of the church's purpose on earth, to bring joy to the world as the consummation of God's will. Figuratively, Zion represents that consummation.

Whatever events are fulfilled embracing the physical Zion or Jerusalem, the spiritual destiny of the world relates to the metaphysical, and the unseen but dynamic forces of the Holy Spirit, gathering people in all corners of the earth. You see what this means. It means that people, in distant glens in Scotland. in mountain villages in Peru, on lonely wheat farms on the Canadian prairies, or in isolated towns on the flat steppes of the Russia, in fishing communities along the maritime coasts of every continent, or rural villages of Africa, can be part of the rejoicing of Zion, as much as those thousands who may gather together physically in the urban density of world population centres like London, Paris, New York, Moscow or Seoul.

> Jesus said to the woman of Samaria, *'...the hour cometh, when ye shall neither in this mountain, nor yet at Jerusalem, worship the Father.... But the hour cometh, and now is, when the true worshippers shall worship the Father in spirit and in truth'.* (John 4:21-23)

Thus the glorious statements about Zion or Jerusalem, in the Hebrew revelation, have an expanded global application in the Christian consummation through the coming of the Messiah, Jesus Christ. Christians feed on the Hebrew Scriptures because they see Christ in them. For Jesus reminded people that he came, as the Son of God, to fulfil these same Scriptures with all their glorious promises in the new Covenant of Grace. It is with this perspective we savour the global significance of passages such as this, 'The joy of the whole earth is Mount Zion' (Psalm 48:2).

Psalm 126 draws us into the rest of Scripture by speaking about Zion. The church's purpose of bringing joy to the world leads us to the warehouse of spiritual treasures stored in the Old and New Testaments. You will recall that we may liken the Book of Psalms to a supermarket, where all our spiritual human needs are met by the provisions of God's grace. In the Second Book of Chronicles, chapter 30, believed to have been written by Ezra, we see a wonderful sequence of therapy which can be followed in every age of the church, even as we contemplate the beginning of the third millennium, since Jesus was born among men.

A Formula for Joy

The sequence is a working formula which never fails, as long as it is followed obediently and humbly before the Lord. The narrative tells how King Hezekiah returned to the Lord, not only personally but also in his role of political leadership, in bringing reform in Jerusalem.

First, he prayed: Prayer is the prelude to great things. Prayer distinguishes man from other animals. Prayer reflects the co-operative partnership of God and man. No person, in whatever circumstances in any place on earth, can ever be really alone, if he uses the cellular communication system of prayer to the Throne of Mercy. It was not enough that King Hezekiah was a devout, God-fearing man. His name means 'God is my strength'; he had to fulfil his responsibilities on the side of righteousness as an individual and in the role given to him as the nation's leader. Listen to his petition, 'May the good Lord pardon everyone...' (2 Chronicles 30:18). The prayer implies penitence or repentance, for only when we know we have sinned do we ask for pardon.

Secondly, he had the right disposition: We note that the person who would know this progressive joy must be rightly disposed towards God. The prayer continues, '... that preparcth his heart to seek the Lord' (verse 19). This involves reflection, taking stock. We give time to make a spiritual appraisal of ourselves. We come aside like a ship out of the busy channel and seek a quiet anchorage or harbour, and review our situation. Yes, when we have made an inventory and realise we are found 'wanting', we are then disposed to come humbly to the Lord with nothing but a request for God's mercy, and that the Holy Spirit might do a work of grace in our hearts.

It is all of God's doing, that is what 'grace' means.

This requires prayer, penitence and preparation of heart on our part. But then it is gloriously worthwhile. Preparation means making ourselves ready for the efficacy of Redeeming Love through the Atoning Work of Christ, to transform us and to give us to know progressive joy. For this great and precious work, we must be disposed towards God and the overtures of His grace. We are made willing in a day of His power. For it is God, who loved us before the foundation of the world in his elective love, who also prepares the heart, and disposes us to receive him.

Thirdly, King Hezekiah received God's answer: 'And the Lord hearkened and healed the people' (2 Chronicles 30:20). When the Lord visits people who seek him with their whole heart, he heals them. Healing power flows through the mind, soul and body. The heart with all the emotions charged with spiritual power, spreads the healing in a glorious capitulation of all our faculties to the work of God. We are called to literally let God do his work of grace in us. When there is that disposition, that submission of our will to

God's will, the work of God is a saving and transforming work in which joy fills the heart, so that the soul rejoices through all the senses in this glorious experience of Christ's saving power. We bathe, as it were, in the living waters of Grace so that our whole being experiences the ecstasy of pure joy. This is the 'unspeakable gift' that the church presents to the world, to all the 'whosoever wills.'

The Necessity of Instruction

Now that grace has won the soul with the power of a new affection, this new experience must be fortified with knowledge. Listen to Ezra as he records what followed in the saving sequence of divine therapy.

'... The Levites that taught the good knowledge of the Lord, ...offering peace offerings, and making confession unto the Lord God of their fathers' (II Chronicles 30:22). This learning was not a dull compulsory duty imposed upon the people old or young. How do we know? We know this because Ezra the journalist goes on to say that the people joined in the services of worship with gladness. 'And the whole assembly took counsel to keep other seven days: and they kept other seven days with gladness' (II Chronicles 30:23). And we are told that there was great joy, the like of which had not been known in living memory. 'So there was great joy in Jerusalem: for since the time of Solomon, the son of David, king of Israel, there was not the like in Jerusalem' (II Chronicles 30:26). Then followed a unity of nation and church, demonstrating a mutual goal of seeking righteousness. 'Then the priests and the Levites arose and blessed the people: and their voice was heard, and their prayer came up to his holy dwelling place even unto heaven' (II Chronicles

30:27). You see righteousness and rejoicing go together, and as righteousness is inseparable from the 'paths of righteousness', so rejoicing is inseparable from living in communion with God. 'For man's chief end is to glorify God and enjoy him forever' (Westminster Shorter Catechism).

11

Jesus and Joy

In the New Testament, joy, the transcendent joy that makes believers delight in the Lord Jesus, is seen again and again. It is represented as the word 'chara'. 'Chara' is that communicable grace which derives from Christ dwelling in believers, and it never becomes obsolete. It is a gift of the Spirit, freely bestowed upon believers. But we should always remember that it is an accompaniment of faithfulness, and the corollary of staying close to Christ. You can understand that, when you remember that Agape and God are interchangeable, and Christ is Agape, expressed in human terms.

There is a heightened desire for joy in those who are born of the Spirit of God. In fact a believer is almost selfish in his desire for the joy of knowing the Lord, and the believer's Lord is the Creator.

And the believer knows God the Creator, in the 'face of Jesus Christ'. That 'knowing' can no more be captured in words, than the knowing of a mother when she sees her child, or the knowing of the child when it sees its mother. Joy expresses complete satisfaction when we are in Christ and Christ is in us, and that joy fills every compartment of our being. There are no rooms or areas reserved for any other god or person. Christ permeates the whole being. Joy is the holy accompaniment of living in the paths of righteousness for His name's sake. David links true joy to righteousness and the indwelllng presence of the Lord. 'Thou wilt shew me the paths of life: in thy presence is fullness of joy; at thy right hand are pleasures for ever more' (Psalm 16:11). The life is flooded with light, and joy describes the complete peace of the Lord Jesus Christ which fills the person from top to toe. It's not that the believer is passive. Rather joy is an emotion that accompanies dynamic spiritual activity in the person's life. The believer is energized in mind, heart (emotions), soul and will. There can be joy when a person is doing a difficult task. The joy relates to the abiding presence of the Master, and the peace that accompanies faithfulness and obedience to God's will. You could say that joy becomes full when a work of grace, apart from the transformation that makes him a 'new creature,' becomes productive. We take in by grace from heaven, and give out by service and witness as productive believers in the context of our generation.

Sometimes people have a great work of grace in their hearts, but profess to have little joy. Why is this so?

There may be several reasons for this but among them may be this, that they have not gone on to be productive Christians in a practical, needy world which cries out for their input and service.

On the other hand, people who may have a very limited consciousness of a work of grace in their hearts, are filled with joy, because they are continually giving out as profitable Christians. That joy as an authentic spiritual emotion of the heart and of which we spoke in the context of the Hebrew exiles returning to where they belonged, is generically the same as that seen in the New Testament. To seek that joy as a social personal fulfillment in pure pragmatism, with deliberate avoidance, if not outright rejection, of Jesus Christ and his Finished Work of redemption, is to miss the point. When the pragmatic task or involvement is over, the person ceases to have the source of joy. Whereas the believer retains joy through his standing of reconciliation and communion with the Lord. Pragmatic involvement or dramatic service are not of themselves a substitute for Christ's transforming power and knowing the 'love of Christ that passeth knowledge'. Christians can rejoice always. If oppression, ill-health, old age, infirmity, domestic commitment, physical or mental handicap or other apparent impediment restrict or prevents us from 'giving out', in accepted callings of service, or working in dramatic rescue missions in crisis situations of human need, this authentic joy of the Lord is still our possession. For this joy is long-term, it is eternal.

Christ's birth and joy

Listen to what happened in the darkness of the night as shepherds cared for their sheep.

> *And, lo, the angel of the Lord came upon them, and the glory of the Lord shone round about them: and they were sore afraid. And the angel said unto them, Fear not: for behold, I bring you good tidings of great joy, which shall be to all people. For unto you is born this day in the city of David, a Saviour, which is Christ the Lord.* (Luke 2:9,10)

You see how the shepherds were told that this great *joy* was directly linked to the birth of Christ, and that this great *joy* was for *all* people. It is a worthy goal of life to seek *full* satisfaction, *so* that our beings experience this *completeness* of positive spirituality, the co-ordinated harmony of mind, *soul* and body, with the emotion *of* dynamic *joy* filling our beings, *so* that bluntly, we 'feel good'. Why bother looking elsewhere for satisfaction. It is here in the message of the Incarnation, or God coming into the world, waiting to be appropriated by all who 'return home'. The shepherds were witness to the angel and believed and obeyed and went to Bethlehem, and true enough they found the child born in a stable, to Joseph and Mary. What did they do then? They went back to their work, looking after their sheep. But it was with a difference. They had been touched by heaven, and something of that 'great *joy*' filled their hearts. 'And the shepherds returned, glorifying and praising God for *all* the things that they had heard and seen, as it was told unto them'. (Luke 2:20).

Christ's death and joy

We all know almost instinctively that we have peace of mind when we do the 'right thing'. Often circumstances dictate what the 'right thing' or duty is for each one of us. Yet outward circumstances are not the only criteria. There are many 'do-gooders' who interfere in other people's business, who, although they mean well, are not suited or equipped for the role they undertake. It is a fine point which relates not only to the challenge of circumstances, but also to self knowledge: what are our gifts, what is our particular grace, why should we undertake a task in preference to someone else who may be on the spot at the time! Of course there are the exceptional occasions. We all know when a need is so evident and we are the only one, however imperfect, who can fill that need at the time. Many believers are diffident in witnessing or engaging in practical evangelism, because there is a stigma attached to proselytising, as if it could possibly be negative in any way to spread good news. But that's the way the devil perverts perspectives in order to suppress the Gospel and prevent people coming to find true joy. We are not really autonomous, or free agents without reference to the context of our lives, our talents, the grace bestowed upon us through the Spirit, as well as the challenges and needs of our day. By nature we want to avoid obligation and have a tendency to believe that happiness is found by getting out of obligation to others. If only we convince ourselves that we do not know the 'right thing' to do, we think that we can make up for quality of joy by quantity, even the pleasures of sin. The trouble is that doing the 'right thing' is costly, when we see it clearly as mandatory for us personally. When we consider our Lord's death, he was faced with the same issues. He had to do the 'right thing' for him in reference to his mission as the Saviour and the ruins of a broken and a sinful world. But that 'right thing' was also linked to joy. 'Who for the joy that was set before him, endured the Cross' (Hebrews 12:2). You see how it was with Jesus. He had to wrestle with the same question - could he find fulfilment without doing the 'right thing', even going to the Cross?

Could he fill his life with alternative great exploits as a political leader? Why, he was tempted to use his gifts to gain an earthly throne and build an earthly kingdom, where multitudes would bow at his feet. But the cost would be that he would have to avoid what he knew in his heart to be his duty, the 'right thing' for him. And let heaven and earth rejoice, for Jesus turned his face to Jerusalem, to betrayal, to judgement, to mockery, to condemnation, to shame, to agony, to death on a hill outside the city wall. His fearless condemnation of sin in that triple combination of 'meekness, truth and righteousness' as the only Begotten of the Father would lead to his death. He had to witness to the truth, for he knew that there was no escape from facing who he was and therefore what he had to do. His joy was to obey, to do the will of the Father. 'To this end was I born, and for this cause came I into the world, that I should bear witness unto the truth' (John 18:37). That was his life role and in his death that mission would be accomplished as a proof of his great love for the world. He gave his life, but in doing so, he would also rejoice in both knowing that he was doing the 'right thing' for him and in the glorious result, in 'bringing many sons unto glory'. That is why we come again and again to the Cross, and see in the Finished Work of our Saviour's death, the crossroads for each one of us, and the very fulcrum of history for all mankind.

Christ's Resurrection and joy

We see the impact the risen Lord had upon the disciples before his Ascension:

> *And it came to pass, while he blessed them, he was parted from them, and carried up into heaven. And they worshipped him, and returned to Jerusalem with great joy.* (Luke 24:51,52)

The disposition of the disciples changed completely. Calvary had seemed to them the collapse of their hopes. From being defeated, demoralised and dejected followers of a lost cause, they were transformed into dynamic messengers of God's redemptive love through the risen power of their Lord. You see how events exceeded all their expectations. Joy arises from the fulfilment of great expectations. When things turn out beyond expectations, beyond what we even dreamed of, then joy overflows. The heart is full to overflowing, so that joy spills out and affects other people. It is as if we carry the joy like an infection wherever we go. We become carriers, messengers of joy, just what God has designed all of us to be. Even as the Saviour was lifted up to sit at the right hand of the Father, there was no sorrow on the part of his disciples. On the contrary, they returned to Jerusalem with great joy to await the coming of the Holy Spirit and prepare to implement the great commission, namely to preach the 'good news' of the Cross, as the 'power of God unto salvation to everyone that believeth' (Romans 1:16).

The secret of keeping this joy

Jesus built up his disciples during his teaching ministry on earth. He had told them many things, using different teaching methods, such as parables, question and answer, illustrations from nature, and by repeated reference to the Old Testament doctrinal and historical background with which they as Jews were familiar in their upbringing.

Shortly before his death he spoke to them using a wonderful analogy, where he likened himself to a vine and his disciples to branches. He placed himself alongside them, calling them his friends and illustrating that he was mediator and personification of the power and love of God, where the Father looked upon him and the disciples for the fruits of righteousness. At this point he says to his disciples, 'These things have I spoken to you, that my joy might remain in you, and that your joy might be full' (John 15:11). He wanted the joy of redemptive love to last in their lives, to stay with them till journey's end and then for evermore. Two conditions are suggested for this joy to remain with them always. He says to them, 'Abide in me'. In other words, never go it alone, never break off the commitment you made when you first believed, never break away as separate branches from me, the vine, which the Father has planted in the vineyard of his church to bring forth righteousness.

Secondly, He says: 'Do my will, obey my commandments.' You see abiding in Christ and obeying Christ's commandments are woven together as God's will and God's way for disciples. We keep God's commandments because we are 'in Christ' as branches of the vine. We abide 'in Christ' as we do his commandments, in bearing fruits of righteousness.

Jesus did not want his disciples to have a poor, puny, pathetic powerless faith. He did not want them to have a feeble witness, with a spiritual life that made them underpowered, like a car with a poor little engine that could not climb a hill. He wanted them as he wants us to have a dynamic faith, mighty, with a Christian witness that is positive and full of conviction and assurance, and a life of service which is lived in full, what ever we set our minds to do, 'with a single eye to the glory of God'. That's it, he wants us to have a full-blooded life, so that our joy might be full.

Faith and joy

We all know what it is to make mistakes, to be utterly shattered by some experience, either through our own fault or the fault of others. Believers are not different from others in this respect but they have a compensating factor. They rely on God's mercy and trust in his forgiving love.

Therefore they do not go down hill because of a negative or shattering experience at one point in their lives. Peter is a good example. He was so shattered when he thought Jesus was a failure, that he cursed and denied three times that he even knew Jesus. But that was not the end of Peter's faith. Peter was humbled by that shattering experience of sin and shame, that mirror of his own weakness, but Christ looked at him with the look of non-condemnation, the look which said, 'Peter, I forgive you; I'm banking on you to rise out of the ashes of failure and be my right hand witness in your generation, as an apostle of the Jews.' And thus we find Peter, a mighty witness to the power of God and one who draws us to the Cross with his tender thoughts of Christ's redeeming love. Listen to Peter encouraging believers to endure persecution for their faith in the Risen Lord.

> *Whom having not seen, ye love; in whom*
> *though now ye see him not, yet believ-*
> *ing, ye rejoice with joy unspeakable and*
> *full of glory.* (I Peter 1:8)

Is that not a wonderful encouragement to all believers, illustrating the joy that is linked to a living faith!

It is not that Peter is praising suffering as some kind of negative virtue. Heaven is to be desired because there will be no suffering. Peter makes it clear that joy and rejoicing are linked only to suffering which meets the Christian in the course of his witness to Jesus Christ.

> *.... rejoice, inasmuch as ye are partak-*
> *ers of Christ's suffering; that when his*
> *glory shall be revealed, ye may be glad*
> *also with exceeding joy.... But let none*
> *of you suffer as a murderer, or a thief,*
> *or as an evildoer, or as a busybody in*
> *other men's matters. Yet if any man suf-*
> *fer as a Christian, let him not be*

*ashamed; but let him glorify God on this
behalf.*   (1 Peter 4:13, 15, 16)

As we sing Psalm 126, or meditate upon it, we realize that it is God who brings us back; it is God that restores us; it is God that makes our dreams come true. Elective love knew us when we were in our mother's womb. Jesus reminded his disciples that they had not chosen him, but that he had chosen them. Who can fathom the mystery of God calling sinners effectually, and sanctifying them to be vessels of his grace! All we know is that this work of the Spirit is going on all the time, adding to the church, such as are being saved. Listen to this, 'The Lord is my strength and my song, and is become my salvation. The voice of rejoicing and salvation is in the tabernacles of the righteous...' (Psalm 118:14,15). What more could anyone want! When faith in Christ takes root in you, nourish it and care for it, using the means of grace, studying God's Word, worshipping the Lord, and working for Christ's cause.

What a glorious formula for joy this is, indeed for life itself, returning to the fellowship and love of our heavenly Father, with our sins washed in the Blood of the Lamb. No one can take this joy we have in believing from us, and no power, seen or unseen can separate us from that love in Christ Jesus our Lord. Have you doubts? Do not think you are unique—even the great John the Baptist was tempted to doubt, while he was shut up in the darkness of Herod's prison. But God has given us the Scriptures, the fellowship of believers, the communion of the Holy Spirit, to make us rejoice and live the life more abundant. So that our cup can overflow with joy when the sun shines, but also when clouds darken our lives with adversity, we are assured that the Redemptive Covenant of Elective Love, will never be broken, and that not one of those who are called effectually by God's saving power, will be lost.

Listen to the prince of the apostles, writing that greatest of epistles.

> *Who shall separate us from the love of Christ? Shall tribulation, or distress, or persecution, or famine, or nakedness, or peril, or sword? Nay, in all these things, we are more than conquerors through him that loved us. For I am persuaded that neither death, nor life, nor angels, nor principalities, nor powers, nor things present, nor things to come, nor height, nor depth, nor any other creature, shall be able to separate us from the love of God, which is in Christ Jesus our Lord.*

(Romans 8:35, 37-39)

12

Journey's End

We must draw to a close. Here is not the end, like the end of a story. Rather this little devotional treatise, is only an excerpt from the log book of one who sails by the star of Bethlehem, and who knows that the best is yet to be. Therefore there is no anti-climax after reading this. Here is a still from the record of the journey. And this can be an excerpt from your life story too. Are you looking for real joy? It is found only when we live in Christ, and Christ lives in us. You see, this joy is an inward emotion, which fills the soul with a sense of the Eternal. It comes from God's Spirit pervading our beings, with all the therapy of being continually made whole, through the power of the Resurrection of Christ Jesus.

This joy is spiritual, and shines like light, shining through the windows of the Scriptures and the fellowship of the church, as we participate in the partnership of service, wherever that may be, in the providence of God.

This joy leads to rejoicing. There may well be weeping for a season, or for seasons, but there will always be a break in the clouds, however overcast the sky of our life may be. And when these breaks come, the Sun of Righteousness shines, with healing in his wings.

Hear the Psalmist in the last verse of the psalm before us, 'He that goeth forth and weepeth, bearing precious seed, shall doubtless come again with rejoicing, bringing his sheaves with him.'

This joy begins as we turn to the Lord, but only when we come to Zion, the eternal city of the redeemed, will there be everlasting joy. In a way, we will have come full circle.

It represents not only the cycle of our personal life, but that of the multitudes who comprise the church of history, past, present and yet to come. What a movement of history, the church, in its completeness, in its ones and twos, coming back to God, to Zion to Christ. For the joy is eternal and is unbroken in eternity. It is before us, not here.

Here there is disturbance, disruption, fragmentation, disintegration. You can go on adding to these negatives—breaking up, dissolution, parting, separation, death. But in the celestial city, there is Christ, and he is all in all.

Here we follow him, whom we have not seen, in faith, hope and love. Faith becomes obsolete, as we pass into glory. It is no longer necessary for it is a necessity only for the journey. At journey's end, we see the land, we enter into the city, 'for now we see through a glass, darkly, but then face to face' (I Corinthians 13:12). Even hope becomes irrelevant, as love is complete. Love becomes all inclusive, Master and follower meet in eternal union. And love, for Christ is eternal love, brings joy for evermore.

Here, by the Spirit, we taste the blessings of the spiritual, as he ministers to us the things of Christ. We taste in a measure love, joy and peace in the Holy Ghost. We see it all, as a foretaste of the banquet in heaven, the marriage supper of the Lamb. All is part of the glory that shall be revealed in Zion, the everlasting city of God.

That is what this Psalm 126 is all about. It spells out the return of people to God, of the church, of the prodigal, of those, who were taken captive to sin or slavery in any of the many forms of Godless living, or spiritual separation from God. And while the psalm is sung by faith during the journey here, in the glorious consummation in the new Jerusalem, great though faith is, along with hope, it will give way to perfect love.

That glorious consummation will evolve like the morning light after the darkness of the night. And the day will reveal to the redeemed, all that God in Christ has prepared for them that love him. They will see that not one of the promises is unfulfilled. They will be filled with wonder at the glory of it all. They will marvel at the scale of the new heaven and the new earth, for the glory of the Lord will fill all in all. They will be amazed at the numbers, countless numbers of all peoples, from every age of history, and from every continent across the globe. And even as the individual enters into that world of the unseen, he will also know that there are many places yet to be filled in the history of mankind yet to be come.

Return, my friend, return to the Lord, turn round against the tide. Do not give in to peer pressure that carries you along with the tide or the prevailing wind of fashionable philosophy or irreligion. Do not believe that neutrality is open-mindedness or maturity. There is no vacuum in the sphere of belief. The creeds of the world demand slavish acceptance, which makes subscribers bondmen and bondwomen to this world. Turn round, I say, like a ship, and you will realise that you can set your sails, so that you can make headway against tide and wind, however strong. And if the waves rise too high so that you fear you will be overwhelmed, call quickly upon the Lord, 'Lord save me'. By the word of God, we say with certainty, in a moment, He who is mighty will be at your side, and you will come to know his saving power.

'Then your destiny, is sealed in the Covenant of Grace, sealed with the blood of Christ. And when the time comes for you to part from this earthly life it will not be an anticlimax. Rather that day, that hour will be for you, and all those who die in Christ, a glorious day, a glorious hour of victory. For all the redeemed, when they die, are immediately made perfect and enter into glory, that is, their souls, or life consciousness. We cannot spell out times or sequences of the events of the hereafter. Why worry? Is it not enough that all the promises of God will be fulfilled, and the Word of the Lord, in the compass of all its blessings will endure forever? Therefore, it is enough to know that all the glory will be unveiled before the eyes of the redeemed. You do not need to fear that you will be lost in the crowd. That is part of the wonder of it all. Christ will come and claim you, for you are His and you are proof of His triumph on the Cross.

Then when all is ready, according to the will of the Father, the unveiling of the new galaxy will take place.

Each of the redeemed will have a new or renewed body, a celestial body like the stars in the night sky, except that there will be no night there. Then, as they form the myriad of heavenly bodies round Christ, the Sun of Righteousness, the centre and magnet of it all, the JOY OF THE REDEEMED WILL BE FULL.

When Sion's bondage God turned back,
    as men that dreamed were we.
Then filled with laughter was our mouth,
    our tongue with melody.

They 'mong the heather said, The Lord
    great things for them hath wrought.
The Lord hath done great things for us,
    whence joy to us is brought.

As streams of water in the south,
    our bondage, Lord, recall.
Who sow in tears, a reaping time
    of joy enjoy they shall.

That man who, bearing precious seed,
    in going forth doth mourn,
He doubtless, bringing back his sheaves,
    rejoicing shall return.

Scottish Psalter (Psalm 126)